Once upon a time, you _____
about politics, sex, and religi_____
about almost anything excep_____
this is the one area where we most need discussion, especially with
regard to transforming the people of God. Jerry and Kirsti Newcombes'
book, *A Way of Escape*, addresses this important issue in a powerful
way that will help all who read this book deal with sin in their lives.

Ted Baehr, Chairman, The Christian Film & Television Commission

Lively, hard-hitting, and practical—the Newcombes have written a
book that will help many people wake up from the trance of a permissive culture and return to the bracing reality of Christian living.

Os Guinness, author of *The Calling*

In their new book, *A Way of Escape*, Jerry and Kirsti Newcombe take a
fresh look at the medieval categorization of the "seven deadly sins."
Using historical references and anecdotes, they challenge us to fight not
only the branches of sin, but the roots—and to cling to the spiritual wisdom found in God's Word.

Beverly LaHaye, Chairman, Concerned Women for America

There are *ways* not to be lead into temptation which were discovered by
others who came before us. Jerry and Kirsti Newcombe recall what those
who went before learned and, thankfully, share their wisdom and expe-
riences with a culture and nation that suffer from moral malnutrition.

Cal Thomas, syndicated columnist

A Way of Escape is a timely work that addresses some of the most
pressing needs in America. Both those inside the church and out will
benefit from Jerry and Kirsti Newcombe's book.

Donald E. Wildmon, President, American Family Association

In a culture that celebrates self-gratification and finds virtue in
immorality, Jerry and Kirsti Newcombe's book may sound like a voice
crying in the wilderness. I have to believe that just as God told the
prophet Elijah of old to take courage, so must we. Surely the faithful
Christian remnant has not "bowed its knee to Baal," but will be challenged, encouraged, and blessed by *A Way of Escape*.

Michael Youssef, host of *Leading the Way with Dr. Michael Youssef*

A WAY OF ESCAPE

Experiencing God's Victory Over Temptation

JERRY & KIRSTI NEWCOMBE

BROADMAN
& HOLMAN
PUBLISHERS

Nashville, Tennessee

0-8054-1763-X

Published by Broadman & Holman Publishers, Nashville, Tennessee
Editorial Team: Vicki Crumpton, Janis Whipple, Kim Overcash
Page Design and Typesetting: PerfecType, Nashville, Tennessee

Dewey Decimal Classification: 241
Subject Heading: Deadly Sins
Library of Congress Card Catalog Number: 99-20474

Unless otherwise stated all Scripture quotations are from the
Holy Bible, New International Version,
copyright © 1973, 1978, 1984 by International Bible Society.

Published in Association with the literary agency of
Alive Communications. Inc., 1465 Kelly Johnson Boulevard., Suite 320,
Colorado Springs, Colorado 80920

Library of Congress Cataloging-in-Publication Data
Newcombe, Jerry.
   A way of escape : experiencing God's victory over temptation / Jerry and
Kirsti Newcombe.
      p.   cm.
   Includes bibliographical references.
   ISBN 0-8054-1763-X (pbk.)
   1. Deadly sins.   I. Newcombe, Kirsti Sæbø.   II. Title.
BV4626.N48 1999
241'.3—dc21

99-20474
CIP

1 2 3 4 5 03 02 01 00 99

Dedication

To our parents,

Leo and Ann Newcombe

and

Roald and Gjertrud Saebø

*with great appreciation for their constant love, prayers,
and encouragement, for they taught us a great deal
about positive things to embrace
and negative things to avoid.*

Acknowledgments

We are very thankful to Greg Johnson of Alive Communications, without whose hard work this book would never have been written. We are also grateful to Dr. D. James Kennedy, whose excellent teaching has been most helpful in understanding the nature of sin and temptation. We thank Mary Hesson for her excellent research and writing help with many of the chapters in this book. We also thank the *excellent* staff (or should we say "family"?) at Broadman & Holman, who make the whole experience a lot more enjoyable than it could be. In particular, we are grateful to Vicki Crumpton, Janis Whipple, and Kim Overcash. Finally, we are thankful to our children for their unlimited patience as we labored on this book!

Table of Contents

Foreword

I was born in a different country than this one. Of course, geographically it was America, but it was a different world then. Our nation is truly, as one writer said, going down the gutter into an ocean of slime.

Oh, there was sin around in those days, but you had to go looking for it. Now, we have home delivery. Just like pizza, you can have sin brought right into your house through a conduit you pay for called the Internet or cable television. They dump it right in your lap in your easy chair. They spray it all over you.

Sin is everywhere—on billboards, in magazines and books, and in conversations. Needless to say, temptation rears its ugly head many times and in many ways in our culture.

How can we be holy in such a world? How can we resist temptation? How can we find a "way of escape" that God promises in 1 Corinthians 10:13?

To provide many practical answers to these questions comes this book, *A Way of Escape,* by Jerry Newcombe, senior producer of my television ministry, and his wife Kirsti. In *A Way of Escape,* you'll learn all sorts of helpful insights on how to deal with temptation.

Part of what makes this book so helpful is what it says about the seven deadly sins, which are really *root* sins that often lead to other sins. The story of the rich young ruler is the story of the tap root sin. Now you know what a tap root is if you have lived in Florida very long. Some trees with tap roots have other roots that go out a little bit on the surface, but they have one root that goes deep down into the earth. You can cut all of the other roots, yet you can't get that tree out to save your life, unless you cut the tap root. And with the rich young ruler—to whom Christ said, "Go, sell all you have, give it to the poor, and come follow Me"—Christ is putting the ax here to the tap root sin.

I don't know what your taproot sin is.

- Maybe it's money.
- Maybe it's sex.
- Perhaps it's gluttony.
- Perhaps it is alcohol.
- Perhaps it is addiction.
- Maybe it's criticism or gossip.
- Perhaps it is anger.

To follow Christ faithfully, our tap root sin must be cut. Yet these sins are so deep-seated, they're not easily removed. Furthermore, they often lay at the root of other sins. Historically, the seven deadly sins are the best known examples of such root sins. (In one way or another, they're all incorporated in the above sample list; e.g., if your tap root sin is money, that's greed; if it's sex, that's lust; criticism and gossip are manifestations of pride or envy or both.) That's why it's helpful to read a book like this, dealing with temptation in light of the most common tap root sins.

I hope you take the time to read this book and master its content. This book could save your ministry. It could help preserve your Christian testimony before a watching world. I recommend it highly.

D. James Kennedy
Pastor, Coral Ridge Presbyterian Church

chapter 1

And Lead Us Not into Temptation

It is impossible for us to break the law. We can only break ourselves against the law.

—Director Cecil B. DeMille in the opening
of his movie, *The Ten Commandments*

There once was a man who propositioned a girl to sleep with him for $25. She absolutely refused. He upped the price to $1,000. She refused again. He kept increasing the price until he offered her $1 million. She hesitatingly agreed, "Just this once, though." He then said, "Well, can we make it $25 instead?" She shot back, "Twenty-five dollars?!?—what kind of a person do you think I am?" He replied, "We've already determined what kind of a person you are! Now it's a matter of negotiating the price."

Someone said we all have our price. Certainly to some degree we're all vulnerable to temptation. There are principles we can learn about areas of vulnerability that will help us become more resistant to temptation the next time it comes knocking. The purpose of this book will be to look at these principles—in particular, we want to examine the seven deadly sins and their spiritual counterparts.

> *What the worldly wise say* wrongly *about temptation:*
>
> *I can resist everything but temptation.*
>
> —Oscar Wilde

A Littered Trail

Have you ever noticed the tragic fact that many people fall away from the Lord? Think about those whom you personally know who used to go to church but don't anymore. Think about people who used to be active in the work of the kingdom, but who, for whatever reason, have fallen by the wayside. Some of them may still profess to believe, but their lives tell a different story. Some of them have abandoned the faith completely. In one way or another, they have all fallen prey to the devil's schemes. Even ministers of the gospel fall away and run off and leave the church for "this present world" (2 Tim. 4:10, NKJV).

Consider briefly a few examples.

First there was Tim (not his real name). Tim had a problem with lust. He used to work in full-time Christian ministry in a public and visible position. Tim's wife had problems handling all of his picky demands on her. Tim began a repeated pattern of infidelity. After a few instances when he was found to be with other women, he lost his job at the ministry. Eventually, his wife and two children left him. Last we heard, he wound up in jail for a form of stealing. He had given in to temptation repeatedly, and he ended up losing his family, his ministry, and his reputation.

Then there was Mark. He had a wonderful testimony and was also working in a Christian ministry. Mark was a complainer—although in total fairness to him, he had something to complain about: his employer was treating him unfairly and was taking advantage of him. As a result, Mark let a root of bitterness grow up in his heart. Holding a grudge against those who wronged him, his anger grew into bitterness, and his bitterness grew into hatred. He got fired from the ministry, and after a little while, his wife left him, claiming he was no longer the man she had married. He dropped out of church completely and quit calling himself a Christian. Today, Mark is very successful in the secular world. But he lost his faith, his wife, and his beautiful testimony.

Consider a couple, John and Sue. John has a problem with sloth. Sue is manipulative, not always truthful, and she has a problem with lust. John has gone from a good job to no job, and over the years he has declined from being a decent employee to an unusable one. Sue has gone from one adulterous affair to another. Their marriage has fallen apart, and their kids have suffered much because their parents have given into temptation once too often. These people call themselves Christians, but they have a poor testimony before the world.

The last example is of a man with extraordinary leadership abilities. He was literally a head above everyone else. He used to be close to God and wanted to be a godly leader. But slowly his power and riches made him careless, and he started to be disobedient to God—in little things. Later, envy got hold of him as if he were possessed by a demon; he actively pursued the man he envied. While by God's providence, he never succeeded in killing the man, he did murder others along the way. By the end of his life, he no longer had any fellowship or communication with God. He even turned to the occult for answers. The man lost his kingdom; he lost his family; he lost his faith. The man was, of course, King Saul.

The trouble is, people do not know that Christ is a Deliverer. They forget that the Son of God came to keep them from sin as well as to forgive it.

—D. L. Moody

> *Obedience is so—is so out of step with today's spirit of the age—Zeitgeist. Obedience is just the opposite of what defines the modern man, which is rebellion.*
>
> —Congressman Henry Hyde

John Calvin spoke of "the perseverance of the saints." He meant that those who are truly saints will persevere to the end. The Lord will keep His own safe, for He has promised it. "I give them eternal life, and they shall never perish; neither shall anyone snatch them out of My hand" (John 10:28, NKJV). He has also promised that He will complete the work He has started in us (Phil. 1:6). On the other hand, it is also true that he who thinks he stands secure should watch out so he does not fall (1 Cor. 10:12). We are told to work out our salvation with fear and trembling, and we should never think that *we* are immune to temptation or that *we* could never fall. To think that way makes us prime candidates for the arrows of the evil one.

Backsliding, quite often, can be a gradual thing. Even the term *slide* doesn't necessarily denote a quick fall. It implies a slow move down a hill, for instance. At least it may begin in a slow way. But once the speed picks up, the slider can move at a quick pace. Backsliding begins in the everyday decisions. To walk with Christ is a day-by-day and moment-by-moment phenomenon. Backsliding is the gradual falling away from our devotion to Christ. A classic analogy of this moving away from God is the one where a husband and wife in their car discuss how they never sit close to each other anymore. She bemoans this fact, but he (as the driver) asks, "Who moved? I sure didn't." So God asks us, if we are far from Him at this point in our lives, "Who moved? I sure haven't." C. S. Lewis says: "The safest [surest] road to Hell is the gradual one—the gentle slope, soft under foot, without sudden turnings, without milestones, without signposts."[1]

The reason that backsliding is so common is that it comes natural to us. The world, the flesh, and the devil all work in tandem for us to backslide, to quit fighting temptation. It's as if we are in a canoe, paddling against the current. Sometimes the current is light; sometimes it's strong—like facing the rapids. But at all points, if we stop paddling, we will drift backwards.

We need to remember that as Christians we are ultimately aliens and strangers on this earth. C. S. Lewis put it very well in his classic, *Mere Christianity:*

> Enemy-occupied territory—that is what this world is. Christianity is the story of how the rightful king has landed, you might say landed in disguise, and is calling us all to take part in a great campaign of sabotage. When you go to church you are really listening-in to the secret wireless [radio] from our friends: that is why the enemy is so anxious to prevent us from going.[2]

As we continue living in this "enemy-occupied" world, we have to have our guard up at all times.

One of the reasons we're experiencing so much dysfunction in our society today is because so many people are not only giving in to temptation (which, in and of itself, is nothing new at all), but so many of them want to redefine what's right and wrong (so they can justify the wrong they do). Cal Thomas said, "What happens in a society when everyone is his or her own god, has their own code of ethics, their own commandments for their own life, is moral and eventually, cultural and political chaos. . . . No one can live without rules. No one can live without order. You go to the grocery store. How would it be if every store decided what was a pound, a quart, a liter?"[3]

But we know what's right and we know what's wrong because God has shown us these things in his Holy Word. Abraham Lincoln put it so well when he received a Bible, saying, "In regard to this great book, I have but to say, it is the best gift God has given to men. All the good the Savior gave to the world was communicated through this book. *But for it we could not know right from wrong.*"[4] Amen!

> *O God, who knowest us to be set in the midst of so many and great dangers, that by reason of the frailty of our nature we cannot always stand upright; Grant to us such strength and protection, as may support us in all dangers, and carry us through all temptations.*
>
> —The Church of England Prayer Book of 1662

Beware of the Wiles of the Devil

Temptation is the work of the evil one, the devil. I once heard a preacher say that even though Satan goes around like a roaring lion (1 Pet. 5:8), he doesn't have any teeth. I disagree. The roaring lion is looking for whom he might devour, and many are those who have fallen prey to him. None is immune to the tempter's flaming arrows or to his seductive words.

Satan is a liar. He has told lies from the beginning. Dave Breese says one of the devil's biggest myths is that "God is a Cosmic Sadist." Breese writes, "His most effective work is done—not in saloons and brothels—but in the minds of men. He is a destroyer of truth. He is a liar from the beginning. He is a pusher—not merely of marijuana or heroin—but of false propositions. He promotes an addiction to lies."[5]

The devil lies to us at two ends of the spectrum. Before we sin, he gives us the line about how just this one little time won't hurt. After we sin, he tries to convince us that we can't get up again or give up the sin or that God won't forgive us or that He won't ever use us again.[6]

Whether or not the pilgrims we see fallen by the wayside were "truly one of us" is between them and the Lord. The fact is that too many fall into sin. Many professing Christians also live in sin. By "living in sin" I mean doing things continually that they know is a sin—without repentance or remorse. I do not think it is possible for a true Christian to remain indefinitely with unconfessed sin. Either we turn away from the sin, or we turn away from the Lord. The illustration of the pig and the lamb explains this very well. A pig who falls in the mud likes it and wants to stay there, but a lamb who falls in the mud hates the mud and wants to get out. You can clean up the pig, but eventually he'll return to the mud. The lamb may fall in the mud several times, but he always wants to be clean again. Likewise, a non-Christian (even if a churchgoer) likes the sin and does not want to turn away from it, but a Christian who falls into sin is repulsed by it and wants out as soon as possible.

Temptations Seem Greater in Our Time

Many years ago Christian author Joe Bayly was speaking at a church in Detroit. He said this in his message: "Teenagers today have more temptations to cope with than people my age when we were teenagers." But a woman objected to this point. She countered: "They don't have more temptations; we just had to hunt harder to find them." He had to agree with her. Bayly went on to write of temptation in our day:

> Temptation is in the showcase, on display, and for older men and women, the threat of scandal, which once served as governor on conduct, has simply vanished, even in church. . . .
>
> Holiness is more difficult to define and achieve today than it was 50 or 200 years ago.[7]

Consider how true that is in the realm of lust! Randy Alcorn writes about sexual temptation in our time:

> Newspapers publish invitations for sexual partners. A singing telegram service sends male strippers to act out sexual fantasies in private homes. Rows of pornographic tabloids line city streets, available to any child with a curious mind and a few quarters. Prostitutes,

massage parlors, adult bookstores, strip joints, peep
shows, female impersonators, gay baths, singles bars,
sado-masochist leather shops—they've become a part
of urban America as skyscrapers and parking meters.[8]

He wrote all this before the Internet was popular. Now we have
computer porn available through a few keystrokes!

Temptation plagues our world and bombards us from many
corners. It used to be that society at large generally held to biblical
standards of right and wrong. Now that this is no longer true, many
of the checks and balances have been removed, and it's up to the
individual to keep to the "straight and narrow." We're tempted to
cheat at work or at school. We're tempted to steal. We're tempted
to lie. We're tempted to engage in all kinds of sexual immorality.
And more and more people don't think there is anything wrong
with any of these sins.

Deliver Us from the Evil One

Temptation comes in various shapes and forms and degrees. In
some ways, it is as individual as people themselves, because
temptation is tailor-made for us by the tempter himself. But remember, "No temptation has overtaken you except such as is common to
man; but God is faithful, who will not allow you to be tempted
beyond what you are able, but with the temptation will also make the
way of escape, that you may be able to bear it" (1 Cor. 10:13, NKJV).

> *Holiness is commanded: God wills it, Christ
> requires it, Scripture prescribes it. Holiness is
> the goal of redemption; as Christ died so that
> we might be justified, so we are justified in
> order that we might be sanctified.*
>
> —J. I. Packer

It is not God who tempts us. Temptation comes from Satan and his demons. God can bring trials into our lives but not temptation to do evil. James explained this: "When tempted, no one should say, 'God is tempting me.' For God cannot be tempted by evil, nor does he tempt anyone; but each one is tempted when, by his own evil desire, he is dragged away and enticed. Then, after desire has conceived, it gives birth to sin; and sin, when it is full-grown, gives birth to death" (James 1:13–15).

So we see that from the first sinful thought, the devil's goal is our destruction and death. The slippery slope of sin has dragged many a soul to destruction. The devil and his minions are, of course, angels who fell through pride. They were permanently cast out of heaven. God and Satan are not in any way equals. Satan or Lucifer, as he was called earlier, before his fall, fought against the archangel Michael and lost (Rev. 12:7ff). Scripture says of the devil: "He is filled with fury, because he knows that his time is short" (Rev. 12:12b). Our adversary is dangerous and mighty, but God is almighty, and He can see us through all of our temptations. God can turn a temptation into a learning process and a time of growth for us, so that that which was meant for evil can be to our good instead.

Jesus Himself taught us to pray this way in the Lord's Prayer: "And lead us not into temptation, but deliver us from evil" (Matt. 6:13a, KJV). I've noticed that some versions of the Bible translate a little differently: "And lead us not into temptation, but deliver us from *the evil one*" (NIV, emphasis mine). In other words, deliver us from Satan. That's how I pray that prayer now!

What Is Temptation?

Temptation is defined as a situation and a thought process that cause us to give in to sin. In most cases, we rationalize: "Just this one time won't hurt." "It really doesn't matter if I do it." "No one will know if I do it just this once." We can also convince ourselves that it really isn't a sin at all, or, if it is, it's such a little one—after all, everybody sins at some point. Thus we talk ourselves into doing something we *know* is wrong. The human mind is a master at justification and can justify doing some terrible things. An extreme case comes to mind. Look at the Nazis, some of whom grew up in normal homes—some had even been churchgoers. Yet at the Nuremberg trials, they justified what they did: "We were just following orders."

It does not take a study of criminology or a lifetime of understanding human frailty in order to grasp the pull of sin. For all it takes is a good look into my own heart to see the depravity of sin and feel how powerful temptation can be.

Sin really means "missing the mark," or "being off target." Sin is anything that contradicts God's will and God's goal for our lives. The will of God is expressed well in the Ten Commandments, and any breach of any of these is a sin. God has also expressed His will for our lives in all of Scripture. When the Lord says to feed the poor and clothe the naked and care for the sick, these are His commandments for us. When the Lord tells us to "go and make disciples of all nations" (Matt. 28:19) that is likewise His expressed will for our lives.

A sin is anything contrary to God's laws and commandments. Sins of commission are the wrongs we do in breaking His laws. Sins of omission are those things we know in our hearts that we

---

One day a grocer leaned over the counter and yelled at a boy who stood close to an apple barrel:

"Are you tryin' to steal them apples, boy?"

"No—no, sir," the boy faltered. "I'm tryin' not to!"

should do but do not do. Elisabeth Elliot defines sins of omission quite well in her book, *A Slow and Certain Light:*

> Some duty lies on my doorstep right now. It may be a simple thing which I have known for a long time I ought to do, but it has been easy to avoid. It is probably the thing that springs to my mind when I pray the prayer, "We have left undone those things we ought to have done."[9]

Thus, sin can refer not only to what we *do* but also to that which we *don't* do.

To give an obvious example: If a person wonders what God's will for his life is, and yet he is a habitual thief, that person must first deal with his sin of stealing before he can go further—for no thief will enter the kingdom of heaven (1 Cor. 6:10–11). This means that a person who practices stealing (on an ongoing basis) or any of the other sins listed in this passage (fornication, idolatry, adultery, homosexuality, covetousness, drunkenness, extortion) will not enter into the kingdom. Or the person who is in the ministry or in Christian service, who at the same time practices lies and deception, is fooling himself and may well be on his way to hell. A person who is continually breaking a commandment while in the church is a hypocrite. The key words here are *practicing, continuing,* on an *ongoing basis,* without even trying to stop.

As Christians, we live with a dual nature, and that will be the case for our entire life on earth. When we become Christians, we are justified before God, but the process of sanctification is just starting. This process of becoming holy starts at the moment of salvation and lasts until glorification—when we get to heaven. This means that all through our lives we have to deal with our old nature, which the Bible calls "the flesh." However, I have found that both success and failure in curbing a particular sin leads to further success or

> *'Tis easier to suppress the first desire, than to satisfy all that follow it.*
>
> —Benjamin Franklin

further failure in that area. Usually, there's either habitual victory or downward spirals.

Victory over temptation comes when we trust and believe that God's way is best. Take the example of sex before marriage. Satan says: "You can have it all now without any of the responsibilities." The Lord says: "Wait—not yet." If we give in, there is often terrible hurt and heartbreak. There can even

> *Character is what you are when no one is watching!*
>
> —Congressman J. C. Watts
>
> *Character is what you are in the dark.*
>
> —D. L. Moody

be physical diseases and misery. This can breed mistrust in a relationship, for if one is unfaithful before marriage, why would they necessarily be faithful after? Worst of all, we sin against God. But if we wait as God told us to, He gives us the joy and security of a good marriage and the protection of our hearts and our bodies that faithful monogamy can give. If we trust that God is right and knows best, He will give us the desires of our hearts.

There are plenty of temptations that can be avoided simply by *not* putting ourselves in certain circumstances. There are people we should avoid and places we should not go. Sometimes we even have to run away because we are not strong enough to handle the situation.

Victory is so crucial to us as Christians, because all sin has negative consequences. Even though there is certainly forgiveness from God for those who turn from their sin and turn to Christ for forgiveness, that does not mean that the effect of our sin will be removed. King David is a powerful example of this principle. Though forgiven for his grievous sins of murder and adultery, he still had to live through the terrible consequences of them. He had to reap what he had sown.

All sin has a negative effect whether it affects many or just ourselves. The most dangerous aspect is the power that sin has to ensnare a person, which can lead to other and more grievous sins. We do well to remember that it is a slippery slope.

Martin Luther said that we can't prevent a bird from flying over our heads, but that we certainly can prevent him from building a nest in our hair. In other words, we can't prevent ourselves from ever being tempted, but that doesn't mean we have to give in. In this book we want to share with you how to prevent any "birds" from taking up residence in your hair—and even how to avoid places where the birds will be flying.

Conclusion

One of the best ways to understand the depravity of the human condition and the root of temptation is by studying and understanding what have been called the "seven deadly sins": pride, greed, envy, anger, lust, gluttony, sloth. These are root sins that were catalogued by medieval saints centuries ago. I call them "root sins" because they lay at the root of many other sins. People who don't understand history have been condemned to repeat it. My feeling is that there is much wisdom to glean from the ancients, from the saints that went before us. That is why we have decided to focus in this book on the seven deadly sins and their spiritual counterparts. That is to say, not only will we explore that which we should avoid (the seven deadly sins) but we will also cover the virtues we should embrace (their opposites). We pray God will use this book to help you avoid falling into sin and falling away from him, and to assist you into personal holiness.

chapter 2

The Seven Deadly Sins
A Brief Introduction

*There are a hundred men hacking
at the branches of evil, to one who is
striking at the root.*

—Henry David Thoreau

Sin is not a popular concept. Rather, it's almost a joke. We have become so worldly in our time that we have redefined time-honored words to justify our "mistakes," our "stupid acts"—our *sin*. Unfortunately, this is even true in many quarters of the Church today. I'll never forget years ago, when I interviewed Dr. J. Allan Peterson on my open-line radio show in the Chicago area to discuss his book on adultery, *The Myth of the Greener Grass*. I asked for phone callers to ring up to discuss "adultery"; no one called. Dr. Peterson suggested during the commercial break that I ask for callers to discuss their "affairs"; suddenly the board lit up like a Christmas tree! This was on Christian radio, no less. Apparently, people today can't "relate" to the old-fashioned, outmoded concept of "adultery" (sin), but they readily know what you're talking about if it's an "affair" (an indiscretion, a choice, nobody else's business).

But a rose is a rose by any other name; or perhaps I should say, a thorn is a thorn by any other name.

We are much more vulnerable to temptation if we slough it off by playing word games—if we refuse to acknowledge that sin is sin. While sin is a rather outmoded concept to our modern society, God hasn't changed, and His Word hasn't changed. And sin is still sin, and the wages of sin are still death (Rom. 6:23). And when it comes to understanding sin, there is a time-honored concept that is worthy of our study: the seven deadly sins. They include sins of the flesh and sins of the spirit. The purpose of this short chapter will be to introduce the overall concept and origin of this list of root sins.

The Seven Deadly Sins

The seven deadly sins is a list of vices that were catalogued by Christian monks in the early Middle Ages (as early as A.D. 600). They are pride, greed, envy, anger, lust, gluttony, and sloth. They are root sins, in that they lay at the root of so many other sins. Although the concept of the seven deadly sins goes back many centuries ago, I daresay if you pick up *today's* newspaper, you will find all sorts of news stories related to people committing one or more of the seven deadly sins! Try it. Pick up your paper today, watch the evening news, or scan the news on the wire services on the Internet and see for yourself. Just this morning, I went through a quick review of the news off the Associated Press wire service. I found stories related to greed (a business fraud), anger (two stories on road rage and two stories on the murders of ex-lovers), lust (a Peeping Tom whom the AP had the fortitude to call him what he is—"a pervert"!), and gluttony (statistics on the nation's growing

> *All the things I really like to do are either immoral, illegal, or fattening.*
>
> —Alexander Woollcott

obesity). Surely other stories had the underlying theme of pride and envy, if one were to dig deeper into the motives of crimes listed. Those guilty of sloth were so lazy they did nothing to grab a headline! I think the medieval saints were on to something when they classified those seven sins as root causes of a host of many other evils, and I firmly believe we can learn from them in order to stand firm when we are tempted.

> *The things of the world consist of:*
>
> * *the lust of the flesh*
> * *the lust of the eyes*
> * *the pride of life*
>
> —based on 1 John 2:15–17

The Bible and the Seven Deadly Sins

The seven deadly sins are not listed as such in the Bible. Yet each one is independently condemned in various passages of the Scriptures. In fact, most of the seven deadly sins have *several* Bible verses condemning them. For example,

- *Pride* - "God opposes the proud but gives grace to the humble" (1 Pet. 5:5).
- *Greed* - "The love of money is a root of all kinds of evil" (1 Tim. 6:10).
- *Envy* - "Let us walk properly . . . not in strife and envy" (Rom. 13:13, NKJV).
- *Anger* - "Get rid of all bitterness, rage and anger, brawling and slander, along with every form of malice" (Eph. 4:31).
- *Lust* - "I tell you that anyone who looks at a woman lustfully has already committed adultery with her in his heart" (Matt. 5:28).
- *Gluttony* - "Do not join those who drink too much wine / or gorge themselves on meat, / for drunkards and gluttons become poor, / and drowsiness clothes them in rags" (Prov. 23:20–21).

- *Sloth* - "One who is slack in his work/is brother to him who destroys" (Prov. 18:9).

These and other Bible verses addressing the seven deadly sins will be highlighted later in this book.

The Origins of the Seven Deadly Sins

The concept of the seven deadly sins seems to have come from the monastic movement around the fourth century. Of course, as human frailties, these sins have always existed, but they were categorized in the cloisters of the Eastern Church. Note what a modern-day journalist said about the age in which the concept of the seven deadly sins was born. This comes from Henry Fairlie, former writer for *The New Republic* magazine.

> In the Middle Ages and even in what we used mistakenly to call the Dark Ages, our concept of human personality was continually expanded by the models, as we would now call them, with which Christian theology went about its work. It was a superb intellectual construction, but it was also a superb imaginative construction, as the vitality of its symbolism testifies in its art and literature. The idea of sin in general, and of the Seven Deadly Sins in particular, would not have taken so deep or strong a hold if they had not reflected a concept of human personality and its potentials, both for good and evil, that was being ceaselessly widened and deepened.

For today, by and large, Christians no longer live for heaven, and therefore no longer understand, let alone practice, detachment from the world.

—J. I. Packer,
Hot Tub Religion

In order to conceive the terrible destructiveness of sin,
it was first necessary that our whole natures should
have been conceived as so rich and intricate that there
is something in them that can be terribly destroyed.[1]

Pope Gregory the Great (A.D. 590–604) is credited as being the
one who officially codified them as the seven deadly sins and num-
bered them as seven.[2] This list applies to everybody, not just
monks. There might well be other root sins to look out for, but

> *The basic warfare of the church is not
> against poverty, racism, housing, population
> explosion, gun control, law and order, drugs
> and what have you. These are* symptoms *of
> the disease, not the disease. The disease is sin
> in the human heart. This is a battle and the
> answer is in the outpouring of God's Spirit.*
>
> —Dr. L. Nelson

these seven have proven themselves over fourteen centuries to be
a rather inclusive list of deadly dangers that we should be able to
recognize and deal with before our souls are in serious trouble.
This list of sins can also help us in defining our relationships both
to God and to our fellowman in identifying attitudes and underlying motives.

Sins of the Spirit vs. Sins of the Flesh

The sins of the spirit (pride, envy, and anger) are more dangerous than the sins of the flesh (sloth, greed, gluttony, and lust).
(Note that one can put greed in virtually either category!) The idea
that sins of the spirit are the most evil may seem contrary to what

Christians often portray to the world; but in that respect we deviate from spirit of Christ.

When we look at Jesus and His dealings with people's sins, we discover that his mildest reproach was for the people with sins of the flesh. Take for example the woman caught in adultery (John 8). He said to her, "Neither do I condemn you, go and sin no more." But to the people who were prideful and self-righteous, He had the harshest and most condemning words possible. He called them "broods of vipers," "hypocrites," and "whitewashed tombs . . . full of dead men's bones" (Matt. 23:27, 33), and He told them that in no way would they enter the kingdom of heaven.

> *The real problem is in the hearts and minds of men. It is not a problem of* physics *but of* ethics. *It is easier to denature plutonium than to denature the evil spirit of man.*
>
> —Albert Einstein
>
> *The heart of the problem is the problem of the heart.*
>
> —Jerry Newcombe

The Seven Deadly Sins and Their Spiritual Counterparts

With the concept of the seven deadly sins came also the development of corresponding virtues. A Christian should seek to develop humility instead of pride; contentment instead of greed; love instead of envy; forgiveness instead of anger; purity instead of lust; moderation instead of gluttony; and hard work instead of sloth.

The heart of this book will be to examine temptation in light of the seven deadly sins and their spiritual counterparts:

- Pride and Humility
- Greed and Contentment
- Envy and Charity
- Anger and Forgiveness
- Lust and Purity
- Gluttony and Self-Control
- Sloth and Diligence

Conclusion

All the seven deadly sins are truly deadly. When they take root in a person, they grow and can bind and control that person until the hold is so strong and the evil thought patterns are so established that all kinds of grievous sins can be justified and committed. We must be aware that we do have a powerful enemy and that his goal is our death as well as our destruction. Can a true Christian lose his salvation? Not if he was truly saved. But if a professing Christian allows sin to master him to the point of total enslavement, then he becomes like the third type in the parable of the sower of the seed. He received the Word at first and began to grow, but the worries of this world, the deceitfulness of wealth, and the desire for other things choked the Word, making it unfruitful (Mark 4:3–32). Is such a person saved? I don't know, but I would certainly not want to find out the *hard* way on Judgment Day!

So now let us consider temptation in the light of underlying motives, namely the seven deadly sins and their spiritual counterparts. Let us watch, wait, and pray, so that we do not fall into temptation. We pray that the Holy Spirit will equip you, from this study, so you will stand firm the next time temptation comes knocking.

Pride

---

*Be not proud of race, face,
place, or grace.*

—Charles Spurgeon

Did you ever hear the story of the woodpecker that was pecking away at the trunk of a dead tree? Suddenly lightning struck the tree and splintered it. The tree fell with a resounding crash, but the woodpecker flew away unharmed. Looking back to where the dead tree had stood, the woodpecker exclaimed, "Wow! Look what I did! What a tree! What a beak!"[1]

The woodpecker reminds us of the many people throughout history who believed in their own greatness, their might, and their power. In this chapter we want to explore the first and most dangerous of all the deadly sins—the sin of pride. To the Christian the sin of pride is among the greatest of evils. C. S. Lewis likened it to spiritual cancer. In fact, listen to what the great British scholar had to say on the subject:

> The essential vice, the utmost evil, is Pride. Unchastity, anger, greed, drunkenness, and all that, are mere

fleabites in comparison. . . . It is Pride which has been the chief cause of misery in every nation and every family since the world began.[2]

> *Pride goes before destruction,*
> *a haughty spirit before a fall.*
> *Better to be lowly in spirit and among the oppressed*
> *than to share plunder with the proud.*
>
> —Proverbs 16:18–19

Lessons from a Great Conqueror

One of the greatest rulers from antiquity was King Nebuchadnezzar II (605–562 B.C.). He had a lot to teach us about pride and its destructive nature. Thankfully, the important lessons surrounding him were recorded in the Bible and thus preserved for all time.

Nebuchadnezzar II was Babylon's greatest king. As a conqueror, he was feared by all. He had crushed his enemies, put foreign kings in chains, and enslaved their subjects. As a builder he was equally famous. He had enlarged the city of Babylon to an area of six square miles, beautified it with magnificent buildings, and surrounded it with massive, impenetrable walls. He had beautified his own palace with hanging gardens so spectacular that they were one of the seven wonders of the ancient world.[3]

Nebuchadnezzar had indeed accomplished many things, but he wouldn't have been able to do any of these things had God not given him his life, his health, his talents, his genetic makeup, his family background, etc. This is true of anybody great or small who accomplishes anything.

But full of pride, Nebuchadnezzar bragged, "Is not this great Babylon, that I have built for a royal dwelling by my mighty power and for the honor of my majesty?" (Dan. 4:30, NKJV).

God was not pleased with Nebuchadnezzar's overinflated opinion of himself. Listen to what happened next, as found in the Book of Daniel:

> *When I survey the wondrous cross, on which the Prince of Glory died, My richest gain I count but loss, and pour contempt on all my pride.*
>
> —Isaac Watts

> While the word was still in the king's mouth, a voice fell from heaven: "King Nebuchadnezzar, to you it is spoken: the kingdom has departed from you! And they shall drive you from men, and your dwelling shall be with the beasts of the field. They shall make you eat grass like oxen; and seven times shall pass over you, until you know the Most High rules in the kingdom of men, and gives it to whomever He chooses." That very hour the word was fulfilled concerning Nebuchadnezzar; he was driven from men and ate grass like oxen; his body was wet with the dew of heaven till his hair had grown like eagles' feathers and his nails like birds' claws (Dan. 4:31–33, NKJV).

After seven years he acknowledged God, and his mental health and kingdom were restored. I remember this story even being in my secular psychology book on mental illnesses. Of course, as I recall, it discounted the divine element, which is critical to the story. God hates the pride of man, not the self-respect, not self-dignity, but pride in the sense of hubris, of arrogance.

How the Devil Became the Devil

The saying "pride goes before a fall" (a paraphrase of Prov. 16:18) is certainly true. In all the universe the most devastating example of this is Lucifer. He was once a highly exalted angelic

> *It was through Pride that the devil became the devil.*
>
> —C. S. Lewis
>
>
> *Better to reign in hell than to serve in heav'n!*
>
> —Satan in John Milton's
> *Paradise Lost*

being. God banished him from heaven because he became proud and haughty. What did Lucifer say just before he fell?

"I will ascend into heaven,

I will exalt my throne above the stars of God;

. . . I will ascend above the heights of the clouds,

I will be like the Most High" (Isa. 14:13–14, NKJV).

How did Lucifer fall? Through the sin of pride. As C. S. Lewis put it, "It was through Pride that the devil became the devil."[4] John Milton in his classic epic, *Paradise Lost,* gave the devil these words:

All is not lost; the unconquerable will,

And study of revenge, immortal hate,

And courage never to submit or yield:

And what is else not to be overcome?

That glory never shall his wrath or might

Extort from me. To bow and sue for grace

With suppliant knee.[5]

Thus, even though Satan has lost the battle between himself and God, and although he's in the worst place possible (hell), he still clings to his "unconquerable will"—this is pride talking. Satan goes on to say that it is "better to reign in hell than to serve in heav'n"![6] That attitude sums up pride in all of its ugliness.

Of all the sins, pride is the most dangerous and the most lethal. The prideful person is despised by God, and "haughty eyes" are among the things that God hates the most (Prov. 6:17). He opposes the proud because nobody can come to God—full of self, with a high view of his own accomplishments, full of his own "righteousness." In fact, listen to what Isaiah the prophet says:

"All of us have become like one who is unclean,
and all our righteous acts are like filthy rags" (Isa. 64:6).

Before anyone can come to the Lord in repentance and seeking his forgiveness, that person has to let go of self.

Clarifications of the Word *Pride*

Today many of us use the words *proud* or *pride* in a positive sense to mean that we are happy, contented, or satisfied. We say things like "I am proud to be an American." Or "I am proud to know you." "I am proud of my children." *Proud* is a broad term, ranging in meaning from proper self-esteem to an extremely inflated opinion of one's importance. In thinking of pride as a temptation to sin, we must think of its negative connotations, which is the way the word is used in the Bible. When we talk about pride, we are talking about a stiff-necked attitude that will not bow and will not give in (to God). We are talking about presumption and haughtiness. We are talking about boasting and vanity. We are talking about hypocrisy and strife. We are talking about *selfish* ambition and love of fame. We are talking about an arrogant and disobedient spirit.

We are not talking about satisfaction in a job well done. For example, it's perfectly legitimate if we say, "I'm proud of my work," if by that we mean, "I'm satisfied at knowing I did my best. I know it's good, and I'm thankful to God who gave me the opportunity and the ability in the first place." But if we say in our hearts, "I'm so marvelous because I did this. I did it all because of my great creativity and superior intellect," then that is arrogant and prideful.

> *Not to us, O LORD, not to us, but to your name be the glory.*
> —Psalm 115:1a

When we talk about pride, we are not talking about joy and gratefulness for all that the Lord has given us. If I say to myself, "I'm proud of my house," I could mean, "I'm so delighted in what the Lord has given me, and I'm taking care of it the best I can." That attitude is fine. But it would not be fine, according to the Scriptures, if I say, "Look at my beautiful house. By my hard work and diligence, I made it all possible! Look at what I have done." This distinction all boils down to one thing: to whom goes the credit? The psalmist puts it very well: "Not to us, O LORD, not to us but to your name be the glory" (Ps. 115:1a). When the credit goes to wonderful me, it is pride; but when the credit goes to God, then it is thankfulness and contentment. It is the attitude of the heart that makes it a virtue or a vice.

> *Pride and grace dwelt never in the same place.*
>
> —James Kelley,
> *Complete Collection of Scottish Proverbs*

Different Types of Pride

We have all come across many types of proud people, but the worst of it is that sometimes we ourselves have displayed some of these characteristics. The *arrogant* person makes aggressive, unwarranted assertions of his superior importance. The *snob* regards himself as better than others and thus behaves condescendingly towards them. The *haughty* person, conscious of his high, supposedly superior, rank or station, displays contempt for those he considers beneath him. The *insolent* person is so haughty and contemptuous that he does and says things to insult others. He who is *overbearing* tolerates you only out of his great grace and mercy—all the while letting you know that it's quite a task, thank you. The *conceited* person has an exaggerated opinion of himself and his achievements. The *vainglorious* person proclaims his fame by boasting and strutting like a peacock wherever he goes.

Pride can be hidden and disguised, or it can be manifested openly to hurt and humiliate others. Some people are masters in subtlety. With a condescending word or a look, they can let you know that they think they are better than you, and that you are by no means in their league. Yet if we truly believed that all we have in this world are gifts from God—including what we are, what we have, and what we can do—then there would be no arrogance. If we could see things correctly, we would realize that every beat of our hearts is by the grace of Jesus Christ. It is when we start believing that where we have come from or what we have accomplished is all due to our superior selves that we start sliding into pride. God condemned Israel for this very thinking when He said through the prophet Hosea,

She has not acknowledged that I was the one
who gave her the grain, the new wine and oil,
who lavished on her the silver and gold—
which they used for Baal.
Therefore I will take away my grain when it ripens,
and my new wine when it is ready (Hos. 2:8–9).

Pride is such a hardening sin; it takes away the enjoyment of life. A prideful person does not want a certain car because he wants to enjoy it—no, he wants it because someone else has it, and he wants it to show that he is just as good, or better, than the next guy. Pride wants to be faster, better, more beautiful, better equipped and have more, just for the sake of showing off.

Pride is usually such a lonely sin. Many relationships have fallen apart because of pride. Many a couple have failed to reconcile, failed to talk things out and clear up misunderstandings because of pride. So they have lived lonely lives with their pride intact. It is said that pride won't keep you warm at night. Pride is cold and hard. Friendships are destroyed through pride because, after a misunderstanding, no one humbles themselves and takes the first step to apologize. In gluttony or lust, there can at least be company, but the proud person walks alone.

Many people consider themselves to be doing a great deal of good in the world by helping the poor or giving money for worthy causes. However, the focus is never off of themselves. They always want a building or some other long-lasting thing named after them, so they will be remembered. Many believe this will give them immortality. We come to expect this in the secular world, but sadly, it is often common in Christian circles as well.

> *Pride gets no pleasure out of having something, only out of having more of it than the next man . . . a proud man will take your girl from you, not because he wants her, but just to prove to himself that he is a better man than you.*
>
> —C. S. Lewis, *Mere Christianity*

Pride can often have many manifestations. For example, racism is a form of pride. The class system of a stratified society is built one layer at a time on pride. Today we even have "gay pride." People are *proud* because of their sexual problems? The causes of pride may shift over time, but underneath it all lies the deception of the devil. In fact, before man's first sin, Satan appealed to man's pride. He said to Eve in the garden of Eden that should they disobey: "ye shall be as gods" (Gen. 3:5, KJV). Thus, there's nothing new under the sun.

Haman and Mordecai

There are many examples from the Bible of pride and prideful people. One of my favorites comes from the Book of Esther. It's the story about Haman and Mordecai. The story deals with arrogance, scheming, deceit, and plans for genocide. Haman was like a fifth-century B.C. version of Hitler. He viewed himself as superior to Mordecai, the Jew who wouldn't bow down to him, though other men in that kingdom did. As a practicing Jew, Mordecai, of course, couldn't bow down and worship anybody; he was in complete obedience to the first and second commandments. Although Haman was gaining favor with the king and was gaining political power, it meant nothing to him as long as Mordecai—who wouldn't pay him homage—was still alive. Haman became so obsessed with Mordecai's lack of worship that he plotted to kill not only him but all of his relatives—all of the Jews throughout the region. Haman built a gallows so that Mordecai could be hanged in it. But, by the providence of God, Haman's pride, arrogance, and plotting all backfired. Before the story was over, it was Haman who hung in the gallows he had made for Mordecai (Esther 7:10).

Hitler and Moses

One of the most evil and prideful rulers ever was Adolf Hitler. He was a twentieth-century Haman. Hitler wanted to rid the world of the very shadow of the God of the Jews and the Christians and to reinstate the worship of the old pagan gods. He demanded worship and praise himself in the Nazi greeting "Heil Hitler!" which means "*hail* Hitler."

Hitler planned that his Third Reich would last one thousand years. He had his chief architect, Albert Speer, build accordingly, as is detailed in his book *Inside the Third Reich*. According to Speer, at one point (c. 1941–1942) Hitler was "totally convinced of his world dominion."[7] And yet his "thousand year reign" lasted a dozen years—only 988 years short.

Hitler predicted that one day he would play a role for humanity greater than that played by Moses. He said, "The day will come when I shall hold up against [the ten] commandments the tables of a new law. And history will recognize our movement as the great battle for humanity's liberation, a liberation from the curse of Mount Sinai."[8] So great was his pride that he saw himself as a new deliverer. But instead of liberating people and bringing them to the promised land, he brought untold misery upon tens of millions of people. And all because of his megalomania.

> *Whenever he came to see my models of the buildings, Hitler would particularly brood over one part of the plan: the future headquarters of the Reich which was meant to manifest* for hundreds of years to come *the power that had been attained in the era of Hitler.*
>
> —Albert Speer
> *Inside the Third Reich (author emphasis)*

The Tower of Babel and Its Twentieth-Century Counterpart

Many centuries before Christ, man proudly sought to build a monument to his own greatness. Nimrod and his followers wanted to build a strong and impressive city in the place where Babylon later came to be. They wanted to build a tower that reached all the way up to the heavens, the Tower of Babel. But God stopped them in their futile attempts because the whole thing was motivated by pride. He confused their one language, and they could no longer understand each other. Appropriately, *Babel* means "confusion."

In the first part of this century, there was a modern Tower of Babel of sorts—the *H. M. S. Titanic.* At that time, it was the largest, most luxurious, most opulent man-made thing ever built. We have all heard the boastful words of some of those involved with the boat: "Not even God Himself can sink this vessel."[9] Doug Phillips is the president of the Christian Boys' and Men's Titanic Society, an

> *Not even God Himself can sink this vessel.*
>
> —Comment about the *Titanic* before its maiden voyage

organization dedicated to preserving the true memory of the *Titanic* and the hundreds of heroic men who sacrificed their lives because of the Christian view ingrained in the culture at the time: "Women and children first." Phillips wrote about this twentieth-century Tower of Babel:

> She was the floating embodiment of the new age of sci-
> entific optimism, and the international symbol of the
> century that would finally realize Utopia. If ever there
> were an event that threatened to rival the tower-build-
> ing efforts of Nimrod, that event was the creation and
> launch of Titanic. . . . Man had finally conquered
> nature. Titanic's watertight compartments, her state-of-
> the-art telegraph system, and her gargantuan size
> would prove this. After all, "even God himself could
> not sink this ship." God, who does not take kindly to
> such gross displays of human arrogance, pronounced
> judgment on the vessel and everything that was asso-
> ciated with her. . . . Many perceived the ship to be a
> modern incarnation of the Tower of Babel. The sinking
> represented God's unwillingness to allow man to build
> any edifice of invincibility or to seek salvation through
> technology.[10]

Thus, April 14–15, 1912 became a night of horror, when doom and death and destruction reigned as a result of man's pride.

Warnings Against Pride

The warnings against pride in the Scriptures are many and var-
ied. Consider just a few:

"The LORD detests all the proud of heart.
Be sure of this: They will not go unpunished" (Prov. 16:5).
"The LORD tears down the proud man's house
but he keeps the widow's boundaries intact" (Prov. 15:25).
"Whoever has haughty eyes and a proud heart,
him will I not endure" (Ps. 101:5).

And we could go on and on. It is a regular theme of the Bible that God will bring down the proud but will exalt the humble.

A Little Lower Than the Angels

Sometimes all the warnings against pride can be misinterpreted by some as a put-down to man's worth. But that's not correct either. God said through King David in Psalm 8:

"You made him [humankind] a little lower than the heavenly beings
and crowned him with glory and honor" (Ps. 8:5).

Or, as another version puts it, we're a little lower than the angels. This makes it clear that our worth as humans is viewed highly by God. Anthony Hoekema, professor of systematic theology at Calvin Theological Seminary, wrote about pride and humility:

The Christian believer may and should have a self-image that is primarily positive. Such a positive self-image does not mean "feeling good about ourselves" on the basis of our own achievements, good looks, or virtuous behavior. This would be sinful pride. And it is the way of the world. The Christian self-image requires looking at ourselves in the light of God's loving work of forgiveness and renewal. It involves giving God all the praise for what he by his grace has done—and is still doing—in us and through us. . . . This Christian self-image is the opposite of spiritual pride. It goes hand in hand with a deep conviction of sin and a recognition that we are still far from what we ought to be. It means glorifying not in self, but in Christ.[11]

> *A proud man is seldom a grateful man, for he never thinks he gets as much as he deserves.*
>
> —Henry Ward Beecher

Conclusion

What we have seen in this chapter can be summed up in one phrase: "God opposes the proud." But does this mean we should not use our talents and gifts, lest we stimulate pride within us? Of course we should. Consider the words of Eric Liddell, the great Olympic runner who was immortalized in the film *Chariots of Fire* and who became a missionary to China and was martyred there. He said,

Love *does not think more highly of itself than it should.*
It recognizes that every gift and talent comes from God.
It recognizes the responsibility to use and develop these
gifts but not to become proud, arrogant, patronizing or
to give itself airs because of them.[12]

That's an interesting perspective coming from him. Here was a man who won world-class recognition for his achievements. Thus, we should surely use and develop these gifts—not to do so is sloth but the key is to develop them for the glory of God, as opposed to the glory of self.

chapter 4

Humility

*I hope you all heard my last sermon on
humility. It was a masterpiece.*

—Dr. D. James Kennedy

One of the greatest missionaries ever was the Englishman
William Carey. In fact, he is the father of the modern missionary
movement. His achievements in India were legendary, but despite
all that, he was also a very *humble* man. He realized that all that
he had and was came from God. When he decided to go to India,
he had no formal schooling; and partly for that reason, the British
government did not initially want to let him into the country. Many
years later, after fruitful toil there, he was invited to a dinner with
British dignitaries. Two officers at the dinner were talking among
themselves. One said with a sneer, "Before he came to India,
wasn't your great Dr. Carey a shoemaker?" Overhearing the remark,
Carey replied with quiet dignity, "No, I did not make shoes, I only
repaired them."[1] When he died, he had made such a tremendous
contribution to Indian civilization that the British government

lowered their flags to half-mast in his honor. Through his hard work, he had managed to bring to a halt the centuries-old practice of *suttee*—where Hindu widows were voluntarily or involuntarily burned on their husbands' funeral pyres. He accomplished many other things for Christ and His kingdom, and through it all he retained his humility.

> *It is no great thing to be humble when you are brought low; but to be humble when you are praised is a great and rare attainment.*
>
> —St. Bernard of Clairvaux

This chapter will focus on humility, the obvious counterpart to the deadly sin of pride. One of the big problems with this virtue is that we might not really want it. Even though we might acknowledge that it's a good and proper Christian virtue, we still hang on to our pride, even if only in subtle ways. Even if such prideful thoughts are only at a subconscious level, we might still be proud of anything from ancestors to recent accomplishments. Rather, we should be thankful for them.

Humility does not come naturally to any of us. Often we find that true humility is only found in those who have walked with God for a long time. That is why Paul advises Timothy not to put a new believer in a position of leadership. A new believer has not had the time to acquire any true humility, and therefore he is susceptible to arrogance and misuse of power.

> *I thank my God for my humility.*
>
> —William Shakespeare
> *Richard III*

Humility is knowing who we are before God. A good picture of humility is King David, kneeling and strong.

Humility was not a virtue at all before Christ. To the ancient Greeks, for instance, humility implied "inadequacy, a lack of dignity, and worthlessness." They equated humbleness with weakness, and as a virtue, they despised it.[2] So did the Romans.

False Humility

Because humility is so hard to obtain, it has some nasty, false imitations. People who are constantly putting themselves down might think they are humble or might convince others that they are humble. But in reality, they may be just downright annoying. Charles Dickens has a character in *David Copperfield* who constantly belittles himself. At first glance Uriah Heep seems humble, but in his constant show of self-condemnation, he was actually hiding great pride.

> *An example of false humility:*
>
> *"Humility is the ability to act ashamed when you tell people how wonderful you are."*
>
> —S. Lee Luchansky, *Look* magazine

Playing the martyr is another form of false humility. Jesus warned against it in the Sermon on the Mount: "When you fast, do not look somber as the hypocrites do, for they disfigure their faces to show men they are fasting. I tell you the truth, they have received their reward in full. But when you fast, put oil on your head and wash your face, so that it will not be obvious to men that you are fasting, but only to your Father, who is unseen; and your Father, who sees what is done in secret, will reward you" (Matt. 6:16–18). What makes all false humility false is that it is still focused on self.

Sometimes false humility is nothing but pride in disguise. Good manners and good breeding are usually gracious and kind, but they can also be cruel when they hide contempt. Someone has said this about it: "Good breeding consists in concealing how much we think of ourselves and how little we think of others."[3] This reminds me of a line from a Tom Lehrer comedy album: "Be kind to people who are inferior to you."[4]

Many years ago there was a revival going on in a small mountain village in Norway. One lady would confess every night what a horrible sinner she was and how she was thinking badly about others. After a few nights of all this self-incrimination, two of the elders went to visit her. The conversation went something like this:

"I hear that you are such a terrible sinner, Mrs. Dahl."

"You heard that?"

"Yes, and that you constantly think badly of others."

"Well, I'm so insulted. I can't imagine who you have been talking to, but I will find out, and confront that horrible, gossiping fool!"[5]

This woman might have believed herself humble, but the fact is, she took great pride in her confessions; and they were not born of a repentant heart, but out of pride.

If You *Think* You're Humble, Then You're Not

Humility is such an elusive virtue, because anytime you think you might have acquired some, it turns out that you are proud of your humility, and so it diminishes or disappears altogether. All humility takes the focus off of self, while pride focuses on self.

Therefore, the key to obtaining any true humility is to center our thoughts on the Lord and on other people and away from self. If we can focus on the idea that "thine is the kingdom and the power and *the glory,*" then we move closer to true humility. In the big picture of things, all real glory belongs to God the Father and the Lamb of God who was slain for us.

Insights from a Pastor

One time, a pastor said to a friend of ours that he believed the most important passage in the Bible is 1 Peter 5:6: "Humble yourselves, therefore, under God's mighty hand, that he may lift you up in due time." At that time the pastor was in his forties, losing his eyesight, and could no longer drive a car. For these reasons he had decided to step down from a large church to a smaller one.

> *Nothing sets a person so much out of the devil's reach as humility.*
>
> —Jonathan Edwards

Our friend was convinced that because of that humble step, God blessed his ministry. Today he is over seventy, can still see, and is still preaching.

Think of how crucial humility is to salvation. We're not saved until we accept Jesus, and we don't accept Him until we see our need to accept Him. "For it is by grace you have been saved, through faith—and this not from yourselves, it is the gift of God—not by works, so that no one can boast" (Eph. 2:8–9). Who can boast because they accepted a gift? How much talent does it take to do that? True Christianity is humble from the first to the last.

Humility Is Not "Doormat Christianity"

We want to be sure to point out at this stage that we are not in any way advocating "doormat Christianity." There is a difference between serving people and letting people take advantage of you. There is also a difference between walking humbly before God and groveling before our fellowman. We all have to find the fine line between being the servant of all and letting people abuse us. (Remember: the key is who gets the credit.) We have to preserve our *dignity* and *self-respect* without being prideful. And we have to hold up our worth as humans as well as honoring all life. My wife's (Kirsti's) Grandma used to say: "Walk humbly before God, but do not crawl before man." Remember George Bailey's nightmare sequence in the Christmas classic *It's a Wonderful Life?* You may recall when he's in Martini's place (which is now Nick's instead) and the former pharmacist, Mr. Gower, comes in. Only instead of being the dignified, self-respecting man that he normally is, now he's a drunk who, along with the crowd, laughs at himself when Nick squirts him with seltzer water. This image captures perfectly an extreme of an abused man who's being walked all over. This is not humility; this is humiliation. To be humble does not mean to be self-deprecating, to put oneself down.

The view of the Bible and the view of the world on the virtue of humility do not line up. Jesus, who was the most humble person who ever lived, taught that being humble does not mean showing weakness and encouraged us to follow His example. He said, "Take my yoke upon you and learn from me, for I am gentle and humble in heart, and you will find rest for your souls" (Matt. 11:29). Jesus showed He was humble in many ways. He asked to be baptized by John the Baptist; He washed His disciples' feet; He ate with tax collectors and prostitutes; He called the little children to come to him. Jesus knew who He was, and the opinions of people did not influence Him. Jesus displayed "a complete lack of arrogance," which is the definition that Webster's dictionary gives for the word *humble*.[6] This definition is correct as far as it goes, but if we are going to examine our struggle to become humble, we need a definition that is somewhat more expanded. Consider this: A humble person is one who realizes that all that he is and has comes from God; who knows that his purpose in life is not to focus on himself; and who voluntarily focuses on God. As a result of being filled with God's Spirit and not his own self-importance, he graciously seeks to serve God by serving his fellowman.

> *The proud man counts his newspaper clippings—the humble man his blessings.*
>
> —Bishop Fulton J. Sheen

Poor in Spirit vs. Proud in Heart

In the Sermon on the Mount we read, "Blessed are the poor in spirit, for theirs is the kingdom of heaven" (Matt. 5:3). "Poor in spirit" should be thought of in contrast to "proud in heart." So, in other words, Jesus is saying, "Blessed are the humble." In teaching the eight beatitudes, Matthew Henry believes that Jesus put "poor in spirit" first because it is "the foundation for all Christian graces. . . . Those who would build high must begin low."[7]

To focus voluntarily on God instead of self is one of the most difficult jobs God has given us. He uses many different methods to get our selfish minds to center around anything but I, me, my, and mine.

Sometimes God humbles us with one blow, as he did the apostle Paul on the road to Damascus. Don Warren, a member of our church, had what he describes as a "Damascus Road experience." For most of his life, he was an avowed atheist. Don had his own roofing company and was so successful that after fifteen years, he was thinking of retiring. But God had other plans. Meanwhile, for business reasons, Don had invited a Christian insurance agent named Brian to his home for dinner. Sitting on the deck afterwards, Don was perched precariously on the railing, and Brian was concerned that Don might fall. Don bragged, "I never fall." Brian responded, "Pride goes before a fall." One week later it happened:

God has nothing to say to the self-righteous. Unless you humble yourself before Him in the dust, and confess before Him your iniquities and sins, the gate of heaven, which is open only for sinners, saved by grace, must be shut against you forever.

—Dwight L. Moody

Don fell off of a roof. He said that it was as if someone had pushed him, even though nobody else was there. He broke his right leg badly but was so macho he didn't tell anybody. When everybody was gone, and he was sure nobody was watching, he dragged himself to his truck and drove to the hospital using his left foot. There he was flat on his back in a full leg cast and still not looking for God. *I can handle this,* he thought. The next blow came in the form of a business reversal; God removed every material thing that was so important to him. Don, still undaunted, thought, "I've done it before, and I can do it again." The next crisis finally broke Don; it seemed that his wife Suzy was going to have a miscarriage, and it wasn't the first one. Finally, he turned to God and cried out to Him for help. Thankfully, the baby lived, Don's leg healed, and he came to know the Lord. He is now a deacon in our church, and he chairs short-term mission trips to Haiti.[8]

Our Need to Acknowledge Our Need for God

You can see from these stories that the first step toward humility is acknowledging our need for God. If we believe that we can handle everything all by ourselves and don't need anybody's help, we close ourselves off to God's help. It is through admitting our own insufficiency that we open the communication channel to heaven. And when we cry out to God, He is always available.

One of the problems we are facing in our society today is one of overconfident people. We have put so much stress on the importance of self-esteem that the result is a false and overinflated picture of the self. This leads to arrogance and puffed-up fluff, without any real substance to support it. A friend of mine describes a person with such an attitude as "a prima donna without portfolio." It's fascinating to me to read about a recent study that found that American students have higher self-esteem but lower academic achievements simultaneously. For example, in one international test of thirteen-year-olds, Korean children ranked first in math and Americans ranked last. Yet 68 percent of the Americans felt they were "good at mathematics" compared to only 23 percent of the Korean students.[9] Thus, the American youngsters ranked first in self-esteem and last in actual skills. This is a result of misguided emphasis on boosting self-esteem without any basis in reality.

A Quick Sampling of Scriptures on Humility

True humility is beautiful, and it is exalted all over the Bible as a virtue pleasing to God:

- "Do nothing out of selfish ambition or vain conceit, but in humility consider others better than yourselves" (Phil 2:3).
- "Do not think of yourselves more highly than you ought, but rather think of yourself with sober judgment, in accordance with the measure of faith God has given you" (Rom. 12:3).
- "For whoever exalts himself will be humbled, and whoever humbles himself will be exalted" (Matt. 23:12).
- "God opposes the proud, but gives grace to the humble" (James 4:6b).
- "He guides the humble in what is right and teaches them his way" (Ps. 25:9).
- "For this is what the high and lofty One says—he who lives forever, whose name is holy: 'I live in a high and holy place, but also with him who is contrite and lowly in spirit'" (Isa. 57:15).
- "He has showed you, O man, what is good. And what does the LORD require of you? To act justly and to love mercy and to walk humbly with your God" (Mic. 6:8).
- "If my people who are called by my name, will *humble* themselves and pray and seek my face and turn from their wicked ways, then will I hear from heaven and will forgive their sin and will heal their land" (2 Chron. 7:14, author emphasis).

"Not for a Million Dollars!"

A humble person will serve others and not think any job is beneath him. I have heard this following story attributed to Mother Teresa. One day she was cleaning a sick, homeless person; the odor was noxious, and the man was grumpy. A reporter who had come to talk with her said in disgust, "I wouldn't do that for a million dollars." She smiled at him and answered, "Neither would I, sir, neither would I!"

We're all familiar with the story Jesus told about the two men who went to pray in the temple (Luke 18:10–14). One was a proud, religious man with a good reputation. He thanked God for how great he (the man) was. The other man was a notorious sinner. In cahoots with the corrupt Roman Empire, he had gouged his own people for filthy lucre. In short, he was a first-century tax collector. He knew he wasn't right with the Lord; he couldn't even look up to heaven to pray. But he sincerely asked God to have mercy on him, a sinner. It was *he* whose prayer was answered, not the Pharisee's. Ironically, we read this passage, close the book, and smugly thank God we're not like the Pharisee!

The Old Testament tells us what a humble man Moses was. "Now the man Moses was very humble, *more than all men who were on the face of the earth*" (Num. 12:3, NKJV, author emphasis). Moses was a strong leader. He is called humble because he kept his focus on God, and thus was able to serve God by serving His people. He was even willing to die for their sins. In the beginning, however, Moses had to struggle to be humble.

In fact, I can think of only one Bible character who seems to have attained humility without having been first knocked down by God, and who willingly focused on God: John the Baptist. Jesus said of him, "I tell you the truth: Among those born of women there has not risen anyone greater than John the Baptist" (Matt. 11:11). He was the first prophet to come along in five hundred years since Malachi, and the one closest in time to Christ. John is unique because from childhood he understood perfectly what his role was:

> *Too often we read the parable in Luke 18 of the publican and the Pharisee who went into the temple to pray; the Pharisee exalted himself and thanked God that he wasn't like the publican. Then as we smugly close the Bible, we privately thank God that we're not like that Pharisee!*

He was to point the way to Christ. In a sense, he was like a spotlight operator—focusing that light only on Christ and not on himself. When John's disciples came to him complaining that Jesus was also baptizing, he reminded them that he had told them that John was not the Messiah; he had only been preparing the way for the Messiah. Now that the Messiah had come, John said, "He must become greater; I must become less" (John 3:30). How's that for humility? Imagine an outgoing pastor preparing the way for the new minister, saying, "He must become greater; I must become less." Imagine if deacons and elders said the same thing. How about business people? Why, this would revolutionize the Church.

The Most Humble One of All

Let us consider that the one who humbled himself the most in all the world is Jesus Christ, and He is now exalted above everyone in the universe. His example should be our shining light.

Your attitude should be the same as that of Christ Jesus:
Who, being in very nature God,
    did not consider equality with God something to be grasped,
but made himself nothing,
    taking the very nature of a servant,
    being made in human likeness.
And being found in appearance as a man,

he humbled himself
and became obedient to death—
    even death on the cross!
Therefore God exalted him to the highest place
    and gave him the name that is above every name,
that at the name of Jesus every knee should bow,
    in heaven and on earth and under the earth,
and every tongue confess that Jesus Christ is Lord,
    to the glory of God the Father (Phil. 2:5–11).

Because we as human beings have such an exalted view of ourselves, we don't easily grasp Christ's incredible humility in the incarnation. But think of it this way (and this is not original)—suppose one of us were to become a bug in order to reach out to other bugs. Even this falls short as an analogy because, as Dr. D. James Kennedy once pointed out (using a similar comparison), the gulf between the Creator and the creatures is greater than the gap between other created beings, In short, God the Son truly humbled Himself when He took on human flesh.

French Christian writer Francois de Salignac de la Mothe Fenelon had some profound thoughts on this humbling of the Son of God and what our attitude should be as a result:

> Jesus Christ is born in a stable. He has to flee into Egypt. He passes thirty years of his life in the shop of a craftsman. He suffers hunger, thirst, weariness. He is poor, scorned and abject. He teaches the doctrine of heaven, and no one listens to him. All the great and the wise pursue him, take him, and make him suffer frightful torments. They treat Him like a slave, make Him die between two thieves, after having preferred a thief to Him. That was the life that Jesus Christ chose, and we, we have a horror of every sort of humiliation! The slightest contempt is unbearable to us.[10]

The true follower of Christ can't help but be humble. His was the greatest example of humility the world has ever seen or will ever see.

Because He was humble, we should be humble too. Consider the case of the poor nun who served the "poorest of the poor" on the streets of Calcutta. Her humility came as a result of her following in the footsteps of

> *An able yet humble man is a jewel worth a kingdom.*
>
> —William Penn

Jesus. Listen to what the *Chicago Tribune* said about Mother Teresa a few days after she died:

> It was her own utter humility that inspired such reverence for Mother Teresa, and it guided her—in devotion to the spirit of Jesus—through a selfless life of good works and charity on behalf of the poorest of the poor, the sickest of the sick, the most wretched of the wretched and the most unwanted of the unwanted.
>
> When she was awarded the Nobel Peace Prize in 1979, she said, "I am not worthy."[11]

"I am not worthy." If she was not worthy, who is?

Conclusion

We closed the previous chapter on pride with the words of the accomplished yet humble Olympic runner Eric Liddell. Likewise with this chapter.

> Humility *looks at its merits, gifts, and talents, but also beyond them* to God, the author of every good and perfect gift, and renders all the glory to God.
>
> Humility *is powerful,* for it is based on the sense of being absolutely dependent on the grace of God. That is why a good Christian has such a serene and confident spirit. Good Christians aim high and attempt great things—yet without proud looks or thoughts; they are not thinking of themselves, but of God. They have simple, childlike hearts because they depend so much on their heavenly Father.[12]

Greed

Gold will be slave or master.

—Horace

During the days of Pompeii when some two thousand of the twenty thousand inhabitants were killed by the erupting volcano, one of those victims was apparently a victim of her own greed. As the brimstone was coming down, she was running toward the harbor to escape by ship. However, she was too late because of her love for jewelry. Not having enough time to find a box or a sack, she stuffed rings on her fingers. She was killed by the raining fire, as she clung onto "her pearls and diamonds, her rubies and sapphires, her gold brooches and her earrings—a wealth of finery that would be placed at thousands of dollars today." Her love of wealth ended up being her undoing; she was overcome by the poisonous fumes and died. Centuries later, "when the excavators found her, she was still lovely, and her hands were still laden with jewels."[1] Greed can be fatal.

One time in church our pastor, Dr. Kennedy, asked with tongue in cheek, "Did anyone lose a wad of bills wrapped up in a rubber band out in the parking lot? Let's see your hand." Several hands went up—in jest (I trust). "The reason I ask is, I found the rubber band," he said, holding up a thick rubber band.

This chapter will focus on the deadly sin of greed, which is as old as time and as current as today's news. Greed can be found among the rich and the poor. It can be found in any socioeconomic group. It can be found among the old and the young—even among babies.

> *Whoever says money can't buy happiness doesn't know where to shop.*
>
> —Donald Trump

Greed Even Among Infants

A college professor was once asked if he believed in the inherent goodness of man. He answered that he had come to believe in the opposite because of the repeated results of an unofficial experiment he conducted. He found that his own twins—as babies, with no training or prompting from anyone—exhibited greed. He would place two baby bottles away from the babies, and they would crawl to get them. The baby that got there first would then grab both bottles and not share at all with the slower baby. This little experiment yielded the same results *every* time. This was the mark of original sin upon these infants. The skeptical professor had to admit that even babies are greedy.

"Everyone" Has His Price

But greed doesn't stop in babyhood. Do you realize that a significant minority of Americans today would be willing to kill *you* if the price were right? These are among the many disturbing findings reported in the book, *The Day America Told the Truth*. This groundbreaking work revealed just how immoral we have become as a nation. Anecdotally, of course, we read about that every day in the news. But this book was based on extensive surveying of respondents who were guaranteed anonymity. According to this survey, only 13 percent of Americans think the Ten Commandments are "binding" for today. Ninety-one percent claim that they tell lies at work and at home—on a regular basis. Pastor R. Kent Hughes wrote about the disturbing results to an intriguing question the respondents were asked:

> The survey also posed the question, "What are you willing to do for $10 million?" Twenty-five percent would abandon their families, 23 percent would become a prostitute for a week, and 7 percent would kill a stranger. Think of it! In a gathering of 100 Americans, there are seven who would consider killing you if the price was right. In 1,000 there are seventy![2]

The Bible sums it up so well: "The love of money is a root of all kinds of evil" (1 Tim. 6:10).

Literature Is Rich in Stories about Greed

Greed is a fatal flaw found in many characters of literature. For example, in Leo Tolstoy's *Man and Dame,* Fortune, the main character, was told that he could have as much land as he could plow in a single day. He ended up trying for far more land than he could ever care for, and after great physical exertion to plow as much as he could, he dropped dead of a heart attack. Thus, the only land he actually gained through his greedy quest was the small plot of land in which he was buried.[3]

There are many stories where the premise of the book is that greed destroys all in its path, including (or especially) the greedy person. So many plots in mysteries hinge on greed. I've noticed so often in that genre that greed, the love of money, was the root of so many of the murders. I imagine that's true in real life just as well.

Certainly the premise of many movies, television programs, and plays is that: greed kills.

A Definition of Greed

Greed is "the desire for more." And there is no end to it. A reporter once asked the elder Rockefeller, "How much money does it take to satisfy a person?" The billionaire snapped back, "Always a little more."[4]

Greed leads us to want things that are bad for us or to do things that are evil to get what we want. Greed is the root of covetousness, which is "wanting what someone else has and going to any length to get it." "Going to any length" may include bribery, extortion, stealing, killing. For these reasons, the Tenth Commandment forbids covetousness: "You shall not covet your neighbor's house. You shall not covet your neighbor's wife, or his manservant or his maidservant, his ox or donkey, or anything that belongs to your neighbor" (Exod. 20:17).

> *I continually find it necessary to guard against that natural love of wealth and grandeur which prompts us always when we come to apply our general doctrine to our own case, to claim an exception.*
>
> —William Wilberforce, Christian statesman

The thing most coveted is money. That is why the Bible says, "For the love of money is a root of all kinds of evil, for which some have strayed from the faith in their greediness, and pierced themselves through with many sorrows" (1 Tim. 6:10, NKJV). Please note that the Bible doesn't say *money* is the root of evil, but the *love* of money.

Examples of Greed

One time when the King of Prussia, Frederick the Great (1712–1786), wanted to seize more land, he called upon his secretary to write up a proclamation of war. The secretary began the declaration in a traditional way: "Whereas in the Providence of God, etc." But Frederick stopped him, "Stop that lying. Simply say, 'Frederick wants more land!'"[5]

A neighbor of Abraham Lincoln's in Springfield saw Lincoln passing by with his two sons. Both were crying loudly. "What is the matter with the boys?" asked the neighbor. "The same thing that is the matter with the whole world," answered Lincoln. "I have three walnuts and each boy wants two."[6]

Warnings Against Greed from God's Word

The Bible has numerous warnings against greed, covetousness, and amassing riches. We already read the last of the commandments: thou shalt not covet. Although this is listed last, in many ways it's actually the fountainhead of many of the other commands. Why do we steal? Because we covet. Why do we lie? Often because we covet. Even idolatry is quite often an expression of covetousness. Seeking to gain something from the gods—like invoking a genie to do what you wish. It's important to note that

> *Perhaps the moral ambiguity of money is most plainly evidenced in the popular belief that money itself has value and that the worth of other things or of men is somehow measured in monetary terms rather than the other way around.*
>
> —William Stringfellow

the command not to covet can be violated without others knowing it. You can be caught stealing, lying, murdering, committing adultery, but you can't necessarily be caught coveting!

In some ways, the command to not covet relates to all of us and all of life because we spend so much of our time making a living—or accumulating possession upon possession. Many women, especially young mothers, work outside the home when they'd rather be rearing their children. But they work because they think they need to. However, in many instances they don't need to pursue that kind of lifestyle after all.

> *Earthly goods are given to be used, not to be collected. Hoarding is idolatry.*
>
> —Dietrich Bonhoeffer

Going beyond the command not to covet, consider the following sampling of the many Bible verses warning against greed:[7]

- "Do not eat the food of a stingy man, / do not crave his delicacies" (Prov. 23:6).
- "A greedy man brings trouble to his family, / but he who hates bribes will live" (Prov. 15:27).
- Woe to evildoers because . . . "they covet fields and seize them, and houses, and take them. They defraud a man of his home, a fellowman of his inheritance" (Mic. 2:2).
- The greedy will not "inherit the kingdom of God" (1 Cor. 6:10).
- "Whoever loves money never has money enough; / whoever loves wealth is never satisfied with his income. / This too is meaningless" (Eccles. 5:10).
- "The sleep of a laborer is sweet, / whether he eats little or much, / but the abundance of a rich man / permits him no sleep" (Eccles. 5:12).
- "Man is a mere phantom as he goes to and fro: / He bustles about, / but only in vain; / he heaps up wealth, not knowing who will get it" (Ps. 39:6).

- "Command those who are rich in this present world not to be arrogant nor to put their hope in wealth, which is so uncertain, but to put their hope in God, who richly provides us with everything for our enjoyment" (1 Tim. 6:17).

And we could go on and on.

The Fate of the Greedy

The Bible makes it clear that the greedy are always punished, if not in this life then in the next.

For example, in Joshua 7 we read how the greed of Achan brought death to him and his household and disaster to the whole country of Israel. Gehazi's greed made him a leper (2 Kings 5:20–27). The greed of King Ahab and Queen Jezebel to snatch their neighbor's (Naboth's) vineyard ultimately brought judgment on their household. It's a long and complicated story, covering several chapters of the Bible (beginning with 1 Kings 21), but the bottom line is that coveting a simple plot of land, among other sins, brought down a dynasty.

> *One day in Sunday school, the lesson focused on the rich man and Lazarus. And the teacher asked the students which person they would rather be, Lazarus or the rich man. One innovative boy answered, "I'd want to be the rich man while I'm living and Lazarus when I die."*

In the New Testament, Jesus warned strongly against covetousness. When asked to divide an inheritance between two brothers, he refused but instead told a story warning against covetousness. It was the parable of the rich fool who gained much wealth but lost his soul (Luke 12:13–21).

Jesus' own disciple Judas betrayed Him for thirty pieces of silver. Later Judas was so sorry for what he had done that he committed suicide by hanging himself (Matt. 26:14–15; 27:3–9). Matthew Henry believes "the only thing that made Judas betray his Master was he hoped to get money by it. It was not hatred of his Master, nor any quarrel with him, but purely love of money; that and nothing else made Judas a traitor."[8] The thirty pieces of silver he received from the Pharisees was the price of a slave (Exod. 21:32). When Judas, in remorse, threw the money back at them, the priests could not put the money back into the treasury because it was blood money, so they decided to use it to buy a potter's field, which they would make into a cemetery for strangers because it was good for nothing else. What a tragic figure. Indeed, greed kills.

Examples of Greed in Our Time

Let's take a moment to examine some of the many ways greed manifests itself in our day and age.

Consumer Debt

Ideally, we would live in a world where some are contentedly poor and others are usefully rich. Ah, but this is not so. We have the greedy poor and the greedy rich. It's certainly true that millions—whether they admit it or not—envy the rich. When Marshall Field IV inherited millions of dollars, he was asked about how he would spend it. He commented that you can only wear one suit at a time and eat one meal at a time.

As for the middle class, of which I am a member, we are greedy as well. Our gold is often the credit card that instantly satisfies our every whim. It is false gold, and it can contribute to bankruptcy. Ninety-five million American families have more than 720 million credit cards in their possession.[9] In a recent year, the amount we consumers owed in Visa, MasterCard, Discover, American Express, and Optima was approximately $315 billion. We consumers have been going into debt at the rate of $5 billion per month or $173 million per day.[10] Bankruptcies are at record levels, more than one million each year. The rate of bankruptcy in the 1980s was quadruple what it was even in the depression-plagued 1930s. Ninety percent of these are "just plain folks" like you and me. Bankruptcy is currently the number one growth area for law firms.[11] These are symptoms of greed left unchecked in the human heart.

> *Let us all be happy and live within our means, even if we have to borrow the money to do it with.*
>
> —Artemus Ward

James Dean and Charles Morris point out in their book, *Breaking Out of Plastic Prison,* just how long it takes on average to pay off credit card debt: "Making minimum payments, it will take over fifteen years to repay a five-thousand-dollar balance on a credit card charging 18 percent interest. This glaring fact is not contained in the fine print of credit-card statements."[12]

The Litigation Explosion

Another example of greed out of control in our time is the litigation explosion. It's certainly true that there are legitimate cases of injury and negligence, and the courts may be the only route for justice to be served. But it's also true that there are many parasitic lawyers who love the dollar, not justice, and who abuse the system with frivolous lawsuits. As one gentleman I know puts it, "We're all just one frivolous lawsuit away from bankruptcy." These lawsuits jack up the prices for everybody in just about every area of life.

Casinos

In the last decade, casinos and gambling in general have made incredible inroads in America, even in the Bible Belt. The gambling

> *It has been said (and unfortunately is all too true) that a young couple today tries to accumulate in three years what took their parents thirty years to accumulate.*
>
> *The one thing couples need to learn very quickly is that individuals must be self-disciplined today. They cannot count on the lenders to force them to live within their means, as they once did.*
>
> —Larry Burkett, *Debt-Free Living*

forces, which call themselves "gaming" forces, have managed to open up more than three hundred casinos in a variety of locations. No longer are they confined to Las Vegas or Atlantic City. Greed is the come-on by which they trap the gullible, who are willing victims of their own greed. Each year Americans gamble away billions and billions of dollars, and it's not just extra money that would be spent on entertainment. Too often, for the compulsive gambler at least, it's the milk money; it's the rent; it's the utilities; it's the college education the children will never have, etc. Too bad such people don't bet on themselves and their ability to make a decent living. Instead they place their bets where their chances at winning are really slim. It's amazing how addicted some people can get. Once for Coral Ridge Ministries-TV I interviewed a security guard at a large casino in Atlantic City. The guard once saw a man who was playing the slot machine fall over dead from a heart attack. His wife who was behind him literally stepped over his body and kept playing that machine so no one else could get to it! Greed knows no decent bounds of propriety.

Bombarded by Commercials

We are bombarded by commercials in our culture. That's not bad per se in that advertising can decrease prices because mass sales, caused by mass advertising, can lead to mass production and, consequently, lower costs. Nonetheless, many ads tell us that we're *incomplete* without XYZ product. They breed discontent and make us covetous. Satirist Tom Lehrer once sang this about the commercialism at Christmastime:

> Angels, we have heard on high
> Tell us to go out and buy![13]

This about sums up the materialistic attitude of our culture.

Missions vs. Dog Food

Too often Christians in the richest nation on earth give precious little of their money for charity or missions compared to what we could give . . . yet another symptom of greed. Missions expert Ralph Winter of the Center for World Missions wrote this a few years ago:

> *Americans relate all effort, all work, and all of life itself to the dollar. Their talk is of nothing but dollars.*
>
> —Nancy Mitford,
> *Noblesse Oblige,* 1956

The $700 million per year Americans give to mission agencies is no more than they give for chewing gum. Americans pay as much for pet food every 52 days as they spend annually for foreign missions. A person must overeat by at least $1.50 worth of food per month to maintain one excess pound of flesh. Yet $1.50 per month is more than what 90% of all Christians in America give to missions. If the average mission supporter is only five pounds overweight, it means he spends (to his own hurt) at least five times as much as

he gives to missions. If he were to choose simple food
(as well as not overeat) he could give ten times as much
as he does to mission work and not modify his standard
in any other way.[14]

In short, we have a ways to go in curbing our greed, which focuses
much of our spending on self.

Conclusion

There are two ironies about greed. One is the underlying
assumption that money indeed can buy you happiness. Consider
what one of the wealthiest Americans, casino mogul Donald
Trump, once said: "Whoever says money can't buy happiness
doesn't know where to shop."[15]
Yet a study of fifteen hundred
middle-aged Americans found
that wealth was by no means
the leading indicator of happiness. The report found that
income was important but not
the most important factor to
"overall satisfaction." One of
the two researchers, Fern K.
Willits, said: "The number of friends living nearby, personal health
rating, frequency of leisure activity and marital status all outranked
income as important predictors of overall well-being."[16]

> *When a man says
> money can do any-
> thing, that settles it:
> he hasn't any.*
>
> —Edgar Watson Howe,
> *Sinner Sermons,* 1923

The other irony of so many people allowing greed to ruin their
lives is that we can't take it with us. Remember the popular bumper
sticker of a few years ago: "Whoever dies with the most toys wins"?
That about sums up the materialistic philosophy of our covetous
age. But it is so untrue because you can't take it with you. That's
what makes the deadly sin of greed so ironic.

chapter 6

Contentment

Thanksgiving encompasses the whole of the Christian life. . . . There are at least 140 references in Scripture to thanksgiving.

—Richard Dinwiddie

Did you ever hear about the ungrateful lady at the beach who had a little child with her? She was too close to the water, and a big wave came in. By the time the water went back into the sea, she realized her son was missing. She looked all around for her little boy and cried out: "Melvin . . . Melvin . . . Where are you, Melvin?" She realized he had been swept out to sea. So she prayed, "Oh, dear and merciful Father, please . . . please . . . take pity on me and return my beautiful child. I will promise eternal gratitude to you. . . . I'll never cheat on my income tax again. I'll be kind to my mother-in-law. I'll give up smoking. Anything . . . Anything . . . only please grant me this one favor and return my son." Just then the next wave washed in, and there he was. Then she looked up to God and said, "But he had a hat!"[1]

Unfortunately, ingratitude runs deep in the human race. Consider the fact that Jesus cured ten lepers, and yet only *one* came back to say thank you! And yet, gratitude by 10 percent often exceeds what others experience.

A Puritan prayer:

Thou that hast given so much to me, Give one thing more—a grateful heart.

—George Herbert, 1593–1632

The purpose of this chapter is to talk about contentment as the main antidote to greed. We'll begin by talking about contentment as it pertains to money, then we'll discuss contentment in general. If you're content with things, you generally won't be greedy. On the other hand, you could own billions and billions of dollars and yet be miserable because it's not enough.

Freed from Greed, by Jesus

Down through the ages, Jesus has freed people from their greed. Take the case of Zacchaeus, who was changed through his encounter with Christ. The chief tax collector of Jericho, Zacchaeus used to make his living—quite a good living, thank you—through exploitation. But when Jesus touched his heart, he was freed from greed instantly. Instead, he became generous. He paid back four times what he had robbed, and he even gave away half of his goods to the poor.

Now let's jump from biblical times to our own. In her book, *The Financially Confident Woman,* Mary Hunt, publisher of *The Cheapskate Monthly,*[2] confessed that as a child she loved money and dreamed of growing up to be rich. "When I married Harold [who was in banking], shortly after [college] graduation, I just assumed that I'd never have to worry about money. After all, a man is supposed to take care of his wife, handle the finances, and make sure she, whose job it is to spend the money, has plenty of it."[3] In September 1982, after twelve years of marriage, the bottom dropped out financially. The business, which Harold had started so he could earn more money to pay their bills, failed after four months. They were left unemployed and owing $100,000 in credit card debts. Mary Hunt wrote:

> During the thirteen years since then, we've paid back the entire $100,000 in unsecured debts plus all the interest and associated fees. I've come to face my compulsive overspending problem and am learning one day at a time how to deal with that and depend on God to meet our needs instead of looking to credit as a solution.
>
> As we've obeyed God's financial principles of giving, saving and not spending more than we have, He's blessed us in ways you could never imagine. The irony is that now I have the wonderful privilege of helping people all over the country apply these same principles to their lives, get out of debt, and learn how to joyfully live beneath their means. It is possible to become responsible in areas where irresponsibility is the order of the day.[4]

Another Christian financial counselor who was delivered from greed is James Dean, CPA, a director for Cornerstone Management Associates and cofounder of the Institute for Debt Free Living. In his book, *Breaking Out of Plastic Prison,* Dean told how he started out as a "fast tracker for a big eight accounting firm." After a while he could not pay all his bills, so he began selling a product in his spare time. After several years he realized, "We were worse off than before we started building the side income."[5] So he tried

> *Contentment makes poor men rich; discontentment makes rich men poor.*
>
> —Benjamin Franklin

teaching for a year. In 1985 he succumbed to the desire to start his own business with a partner. But after several months, "success never came." Instead, he and his immediate family just ended up in significant debt. So they had to move in with his parents.[6]

Dean's father had a successful architectural firm. He welcomed him home, offered him a job, and offered to pay off Dean's debts immediately, on the condition that Dean would repay him at a fair rate of interest. Jim continued:

> The job my father gave me was not high paying. But it was enough. We had a roof, food, and a single loan payment toward becoming debt-free. The interest was reasonable, unlike the charge-card rates more than twice the amount.
>
> The healing process had begun. My desire for freedom from a pattern of using debt to bail myself out led to much time in the Bible and on my knees, asking God to teach me where I had strayed. What a few months earlier I would have considered a tedious unproductive road, now became something like a holy quest. My intense study of God's word yielded ten lessons—about myself and about money. These lessons have served me—and those who come to me for help again and again.[7]

Greed: The American Way?

Mary Hunt and James Dean may not have been what you would call typically greedy, but they were not content with what they had and wanted more. The things they wanted were not evil, so they did not see anything wrong in getting them now and paying for them later. Isn't that the American way? How many of us have done the same?

Actually, it is not the American way. Up until 1950 home mortgages were rare and car loans were for twelve months or less. But after World War II, there were so many ex-GIs who had no credit history but who needed loans for education and housing that Congress passed what is known as the GI Bill. It guaranteed that the government would back up loans made to ex-GIs by commercial lenders. In the 1960s the bankers, who had lived through the Great Depression had retired; the younger ones who replaced

> *If the grass looks greener on the other side of the fence, you can bet the water bill is higher.*
>
> —Anonymous

them were more aggressive and had grown up with a "debt mentality." They were willing to loan more money and for longer periods of time. By the 1970s virtually every segment of the economy depended on credit. Mortgage loans were no longer 25 percent of the husband's salary, but could be 40 percent of both incomes; car loans were extended to five years, some with a balloon payment of 40 percent at the end. By the 1980s many were forced to take out a second mortgage on their homes to pay for their children's college education.[8]

Today people think that debt is normal, but it is not. The ease of borrowing money leads to self-indulgence, impulse buying, and get-rich-quick schemes. The root cause of all of these, whether we recognize it or not, is greed. And I think that is the problem. We are greedy and don't even recognize it. We succumb to greed because borrowing is easy and advertisers tell us, "Pamper yourself. You deserve it."

Contentment: God's Way

Being greedy is not God's way. The apostle Paul challenged us to follow God's way: to "be content." The Bible says, "Keep your lives free from the love of money and be content with what you have, because God has said, 'Never will I leave you; never will I forsake you'" (Heb. 13:5).

Jesus' teaching about contentment is this: it is impossible to be greedy and godly at the same time. "No one can serve two masters.

Either he will hate the one and love the other, or he will be devoted to the one and despise the other. You cannot serve both God and Money" (Matt. 6:24). Jesus did not say we must not or we should not love both God and money. He said we *cannot*. It is an impossibility. Further, Jesus told us not to worry about material goods but rather to seek first God's kingdom and His righteousness and then the Lord will provide for us.

Ron Blue, a Christian financial counselor and managing partner of Ronald Blue & Co., says that to be content we need to recognize several things:[9]

God owns it all. Because He is the owner, He has rights. Because we are stewards, we have responsibilities. It is not only that every giving decision is a spiritual decision but also every spending decision is a spiritual decision.

We are in a growth process. God uses material possessions as a tool, a test, and a testimony. Money is not only a tool but also a test.

The amount is not important. Since God owns everything, He can choose the amount He wants you to have. The important thing is how you handle whatever amount He has given you. If you handle it well, you will grow, and He will entrust you with more. But however much or little you have, your attitude of caring for it should remain the same.

Money is never an end in itself. It's merely a resource to accomplish other goals and objectives.

Debt is dangerous. The Bible discourages debt but does not prohibit it. Debt is not a sin,

> *Avarice and happiness never saw each other; how then should they become acquainted?*
>
> —Ben Franklin

but it is dangerous for two reasons: (1) It presumes upon the future that repayment will be made when, in fact, the future is uncertain; and (2) It may deny God an opportunity to work. Ron recalls that before he started his business, he went to open a line of credit for it at a bank. Opening a line of credit is a normal business procedure for anyone wanting to start a new business. But the more he prayed about it, the more strongly he felt he should not go into debt to start the business, so he called the bank to cancel the line of credit. About one week later, someone called asking him to develop a seminar, which gave him the funds he needed, about $10,000. From this and similar experiences, Ron wrote:

> I am convinced that had I not canceled the line of credit with the bank and depended solely on God to provide the resources, I would never have received the contract to design the seminar. . . . In many cases when we borrow money, we are putting the lender in the place of God.[10]

"Do you say your prayers before eating?" the teacher asked the little seven-year-old. "It ain't necessary," she answered. "My mom is a good cook."

—Joey Adams, *The God Bit*

Larry Burkett, founder of Christian Financial Concepts, well-known as the author of some forty books on biblical principles of finances and for his radio program, *How to Manage Your Money,* believes it is possible to be content with whatever amount of money you have. He calls that financial freedom: living within your means with contentment. He teaches strategies for achieving contentment. Burkett wrote:

> Above all else, God is concerned with our attitude. The abundance or lack of money does not affect our relationship to Him—only our attitude does. The Christian must be able to trust God in every circumstance, believing that He loves us and gives us only the stewardship we can handle without being tempted beyond that which we can withstand. Because of its tangibility,

money is a testing ground before God of our true willingness to surrender ourselves to Him.[11]

The most contented people I know are those who give to God
first. Before they pay their bills or buy anything for themselves,
they make sure that God gets at least 10 percent of their money.
Those who do this willingly and with joy experience the greatest
contentment. They don't do it to get something from God, but
often He stretches what is left, so that it buys much more than they
ever expected, or sometimes He may surprise them with an unex-
pected gift. They are also generous to those who are in need. Like
Zacchaeus, they have been delivered from greed, and like the
apostle Paul, they are content in every situation (Phil. 4:11–13).

The command went out from God: Thou shalt not covet. If
you're content, if you're thankful, generally you don't covet. But as
we have pointed out, ingratitude is often the norm. Let's move
beyond money and consider contentment in general.

I remember seeing one of *The Far Side* cartoons by Gary
Larson that showed one dog in his den showing another dog his
mounted, stuffed trophies on his wall. There were a couple of
stuffed cat heads and bird heads and also a human hand mounted
on the wall. The host dog was saying to his guest, "And that's the
hand that fed me."

Ingratitude runs deep in
the human race. In the 1930s,
there was a discussion among
some friends about how
gloomy things were. One of the
persons remarked, "There isn't
much to be thankful for." But

> *Who is rich? He that*
> *rejoices in his*
> *Portion.*
>
> —Ben Franklin

another one piped up and said that at least he was thankful—for
his encouraging schoolteacher, Mrs. Wendt, from thirty years earlier. Others asked him if he had ever bothered to thank her. No, he
had to admit, he had not. So that night he sat down and wrote a
long overdue letter of thanks. With shaky handwriting, she wrote
back this reply: "My dear Willie: I want you to know what your

note meant to me. I am an old lady in my eighties, living alone in a small room, cooking my own meals, lonely and seeming like the last leaf on the tree. . . . You will be interested to know, Willie, that I taught school for fifty years, and in all that time yours is the first letter of appreciation I have ever received. It came on a blue, cold morning, and it cheered my lonely old heart as nothing has cheered me in many years."[12]

Perhaps, we all have Mrs. Wendts in our lives whom we could thank and who would benefit greatly by our thanks. Furthermore, we know that we owe a large debt of gratitude to the Lord, every day, even for every little beat of our hearts.

"String Bean Tony"

One time when I was participating in the wheelchair ministry for our church, an incident happened that illustrates this kind of gratitude. We picked up about five people at a local nursing home and brought them to our service. Many of them had gone the previous day to a local Thanksgiving banquet where they had been picked up and brought to the feast. When I asked them what they thought about it, all but one complained:

"Oh, we were waiting for hours in the line!"

"It was terrible. . . . All they gave you was this little piece of dried-out turkey—and after a long wait too!"

Another murmured about this or that.

But Tony, the one who didn't complain, said, "The string beans . . . they were just great! They were cooked just the right way! And the fellowship was great too!"

That man was incredible. He was always thankful, whatever the circumstances. Even if there was only one little good thing to be found, Tony would find it!

The Secret of Contentment

Someone once quipped that a man with six children is usually more content than a man with six million dollars. The reason: a man with six million dollars always wants more.[13]

Richard Swenson, M.D., who has done his best to cultivate an optimum lifestyle for himself and his family through contentment, simplicity, balance, and rest, says that it's hard to *stay* content:

> For one thing it is slippery. Contentment is not at all like cutting down a tree, which when it is done, is done. It is more like trying to pick up mercury with tweezers— it keeps squirting away. It's like the carrot suspended two feet in front of our face that moves every time we do. We keep chasing, and it keeps dodging. "Give a man everything he wants," declared Immanuel Kant, "and at that moment, everything will not be everything."[14]

We complain so often that sometimes we don't recognize that what God has given us is just right for us. Two examples I've read about come to mind. One is a couple who wanted to sell their house, but as they read the realtor's ad, they realized that what they had was *just* what they wanted. "We never knew we had such a place until we read your description of it."[15] Another example is a couple that filed for divorce. The ex-husband sought the services of a computer service for a compatible mate. Of two thousand possible names, his ex-wife was selected as the most compatible. The couple then got back together and remarried.[16]

> *Ingratitude is always a kind of weakness. I have never known men of ability to be ungrateful.*
>
> —Goethe

A Repeated Theme in Scripture

We know the Bible says a lot about God's provision and our need to be content:

- "But godliness with contentment is great gain" (1 Tim. 6:6).
- "And my God shall supply all your need according to His riches in glory by Christ Jesus" (Phil. 4:19, NKJV).
- "The LORD is my shepherd, I shall not be in want" (Ps. 23:1). That is, I shall lack nothing.
- "The lions may grow weak and hungry, but those who seek the LORD lack no good thing" (Ps. 34:10).

These are just a smattering of what the Scriptures say on the subject. The overall points of the Bible are these:

1. The Lord provides for His people.
2. We are to trust Him in good times and in bad.
3. We owe Him our thanksgiving.
4. God can't stand grumbling and complaining.

When we have an attitude of gratitude, it precludes a greedy or covetous spirit.

Always Wanting What Is Not

My mom always used to say:

As a rule, a man's a fool;
When it's hot, he wants it cool.
When it's cool, he wants it hot—
Always wanting what is not.

She also says, "If you don't get what you want, want what you get."

So often our attitude is one of whining and complaining. God might bless us in some great way, but because of a small detail, we can't be thankful. We often think that "if only God gives me a wife [husband] or a better job or a _____ [you fill in the blank], *then* I'll be happy and not complain." Want to bet? Unfortunately, complaining also runs deep in the race. Only by regularly thanking the Lord can we be free from our habitual murmuring.

Complaining is a mixture of ingratitude, lack of faith, and lack of memory. Probably, the classic complainers were the children of Israel, who wandered around the desert with Moses for forty years. They mumbled and grumbled continually; if it wasn't one thing, it was another. Each concern may have been valid in itself, but their complaints always exposed their lack of faith. Often we sit back smugly in judgment of the Israelites. "Why, those idiots," we think, "couldn't they recall how God parted the Red Sea for them or how He always provided their needs?" But don't we make the very same mistake? We whine and pray for something, and God grants it. If we remember to, we thank Him for it. But the next time we're in trouble or in need, we pray to God as if we totally forgot what He did for us before. Our memories seem awfully dull towards God.

I offer three suggestions to help us overcome our habitual grumbling.

1. *Recall what God has done in your life.* Keep track of His blessings and answered prayers in a diary. Then when you're in doubt, you can pore over these and recall again how God has been faithful in your life. We have a family tradition on Sundays where we get to track God's faithfulness in our lives. We go around the room, and each family member says what he or she wants us to pray about, and we write those requests down in a notebook. The notebook has two columns. On the left side of the page, we have

---

Let me be thankful first, because I was never robbed before; second, because, although they took my purse, they did not take my life; third, because, although they took my all, it was not much; and fourth, because it was I who was robbed, not I who robbed.

—Entry in the diary of Matthew Henry after he was robbed

a column called "We prayed." The right column says, "He answered." Having it all in print helps us to remember specific ways in which God has helped us.

2. *Meditate on the example of Jesus being crucified for our sakes.* None of us have faced anything like Jesus did, yet He did not grumble or complain about it. He did voice His pain: "Father, if you are willing, take this cup from me." Yet within the same breath, He voiced His submission to the Father: "Yet not my will, but yours be done" (Luke 22:42). Unless you're spiritually dead, it's virtually impossible to read the passion of our Lord and not be moved to thanks for what He did for us, in our place.

3. *Give thanks to God.* Genuine thanksgiving can be among the best remedies for a complaining spirit. St. John of the Cross said something to the effect that a prayer of thanksgiving offered to God in the midst of a crisis means more than a thousand prayers of thanksgiving when all is going well. If you ever find yourself in a pity party, think about Jesus dying on the cross in your place. You can give thanks in all circumstances because if you're saved, you know you're going to heaven.

Consider the benefits of being a Christian. . . .

- We have the promise and assurance of going to heaven.
- All things work together for the good, because of God who is sovereign.
- We can bring all our burdens to Him in prayer.
- We're part of a worldwide family, the largest family in the world—the family of God.
- Life is meaningful, not pointless.
- We know the truth, and the truth sets us free.
- There is freedom from sin.
- We have sixty-six love letters from God in the Bible.
- If we're obedient, we're spared from all sorts of difficulties that strike down millions of our fellow citizens.
- Above all, we are loved by God with an everlasting love.

Finally, instead of thinking, "If only _____, then I'll be happy," why not have an attitude of thanks for the present moment—assuming, of course, you'll do what you can to improve the situation? With an attitude of thanks to God, we can think clearly and avoid the rut of self-pity. Then we can be satisfied when it's hot and content when it's not.

Some Factors That Can Short-Circuit Thankfulness

Cynicism short-circuits thankfulness. When we look at the world through cynical eyes instead of grateful ones, we tend to focus on the negative. We gaze more upon Satan's handiwork than the Lord's.

Worldliness short-circuits thankfulness. The Bible tells us that we either love God or love the world. Whoever loves the world (as in the sinfulness of the world) hates God. James wrote, "Friendship with the world is hatred toward God" (James 4:4). When we are worldly, we focus on the things that are made and not on the Maker of those things, to whom all thanks are due.

Pride short-circuits thankfulness. Pride deceives us into thinking that we are *deserving* of what we have. I'm reminded of the mockery prayer from Bart Simpson in *The Simpsons* where he "prayed" something to this effect: "Dear God, we bought these groceries with our own money which we earned ourselves. So thanks for nothing. Amen." But it is God who gives us the opportunity to earn money. He provides the seed, the rain, the harvest, and all the things needed for food. When we are proud and self-sufficient, then we don't see the need for gratitude. But God is indeed the source of all things, including life itself.

The opportunity to live in this country is something we often take for granted. One time I came across an unbelievable sight at the beach. This was in August 1994 during the crisis when many were trying to flee from Cuba on makeshift rafts. I stumbled across one off the shores of Deerfield Beach (north of Ft. Lauderdale). It's about three hundred miles or so away from Cuba. This raft reflected the desperation that its makers must have felt. It was composed primarily of three wooden doors. There was some sort of Styrofoam or flotsam at the bottom to keep it afloat. One of the doors was at the bottom of the structure and the other two made up the raft's sides, with pieces of wood nailed across to serve as crossbeams. Some of the wood used included wooden shutters. It was literally as if someone had torn apart his own home in order to put the raft together! Then they would have had to float or row over in the treacherous waters, in the grueling sun, with the potential threat of sharks along the way, to get to America so that maybe—*just maybe!*—they would get a chance to enjoy what you and I have every day. Freedom. The chance for a better life. It is a privilege to live here and shouldn't be taken for granted. It is something for which we should be very grateful.

Conclusion

Thus, whether dealing with our finances or anything else, we are to be content, to be full of thanksgiving. Father John Powell, a professor at Loyola in Chicago, said in his book, *He Touched Me*, that one time in seminary, he observed the "Brother Infirmarian" tucking two elderly and ill priests to bed in the infirmary of the retirement home for priests. One of them was really grouchy and complaining about everything. The other was a saintly, thankful old man who looked for the good in everything. Then Powell writes that he was gripped by a sudden realization: "One day I would be one of those two priests: selfish and cantankerous or loving and grateful. But I knew, as I stood in the corridor of the infirmary, that the decision would not be made in the twilight of my life. It would be made in the young, formative years. It was being made then. Our yesterdays lie heavily upon our todays, and our todays lie heavily upon our tomorrows."[17] Thankfulness on a daily basis can make a big difference.

chapter 7

Envy

*As a moth gnaws a garment,
so doth envy consume a man.*

—St. Chrysostom

A home economics teacher held a contest for her high school students to see which one was the best seamstress. The class had worked hard, and the garments they entered were beautifully sewn. It was hard to choose a winner. After a winner was selected, one girl was so envious that she took a pair of scissors and cut holes in the garment of the winner.[1]

We all are familiar with the sad case of the Olympic skater who allegedly hired some thugs to try to smash her competitor's knee.

Then there's the story from ancient Greece about a prized athlete who was so good in the public games that his fellow citizens erected a statue in his honor. But a bitter rival, consumed with envy, went out each night to attempt to destroy the statue by pushing it off its pedestal; he made very slow progress. Finally, he was successful one night—only it fell on him and crushed him to death!

This chapter will look at the deadly sin of envy. Envy was the motive for the very first murder and for countless other murders since the dawn of time. Some people define envy and jealousy as two separate items. But for our purposes here we will generally use the two terms interchangeably.

You've Got It! I Want It!

Envy can be summed up in two short sentences that were uttered by a thief when he held up a pharmacy in Gulfport, Mississippi, more than a decade ago. He held a gun to the pharmacist's head, demanding money and drugs. He shouted: "You've got it! I want it!"[2] That's a great definition of envy. It cuts to the chase; it cuts through any religious games or sanctimonious ways to hide our jealousy: You've got it! I want it!

The irony of envy is that a person may be fabulously wealthy compared to the vast majority of the rest of the world. Yet he may envy that small population that has more than he . . . and that gnaws at him so he ends up not enjoying the abundance he has because of these feelings of envy.[3] Happiness and envy can't coexist. As different authors have pointed out, one can be lustful and happy. One can be gluttonous and happy. One may even enjoy indulging his temper by flying off in a rage. But one can't be envious and happy simultaneously. They are mutually exclusive.

A Quick Test

Here's a quick test to see if the deadly sin of envy rests in your heart: Do you envy Bill Gates? Do you envy the latest movie star? Do you envy the latest pop star? If you're a minister, do you envy Billy Graham? Do you envy the wealthy? I think if we were honest, we would see that some degree of envy resides in all of our hearts. "Not me," you say? But suppose a coworker were promoted this very week, would that *immediately* elicit thanksgiving in your heart or resentment?

Envy is likened to a sickness, and we're all vulnerable to its icy grip in our hearts if we're not careful. From the smallest resentment of another's possession or advantage to the blinding desire to destroy that person, too often envy raises its ugly head and wreaks havoc.

What was the greatest single crime ever committed in the history of the world? What was the greatest single injustice ever perpetrated on any one person? The answer, of course, is the crucifixion of Jesus Christ. He was not only innocent, He was the only perfectly innocent person who ever lived. Yet He was executed like a common criminal.

> *If there is any sin more deadly than envy, it is being pleased at being envied.*
>
> —Richard Armour

What was the motive of those who sought His death? Envy. "For [Pilate] knew it was out of envy that they had handed Jesus over to him" (Matt. 27:18).

Murders Caused by Envy

Emperors, kings, and dictators through the centuries have likewise committed murder because of their envy. Much of the history of England, for instance, contains episodes where the brothers, sisters, or other relatives of the monarch ended up in the Tower of London because of envy, lest they rival his or her power. Many of these siblings were murdered simply for having been born. Consider other examples in history of leaders killing others because of their envy:

- Herod was envious of a little baby, Jesus, who, it was said, was born a king. Herod couldn't bear to have this potential rival to his political power, even though the "rival" was a little infant! So Herod massacred all sorts of baby boys to try to remove this threat to his power. Having been warned in a dream, Joseph and Mary had already fled.

They were safely in Egypt by the time this slaughter of the innocents took place.

- The French Revolution spilled the blood of one perceived enemy of the people after another. Eventually, the revolutionaries rivaled each other for political power, and virtually each one ended up getting killed during the reign of terror. Of course, not all were killed because of envy— pride, fear, mistrust, and hatred were also factors. The whole affair ended as a gruesome and chaotic chapter in the history of humanity and paved the way to the rise of a tyrant (Napoleon) who finally restored order.

- Josef Stalin massacred 40 to 60 million of his own people in order to force communism on Russia, a portion of whom were killed because of his paranoid envy. His envy of the capitalist West was so great that when soldiers returned from the European theater, he eventually had them killed in what is known as "the hero's purge" because they had seen what life was like outside of communist Russia. Consider also his murder of all his former colleagues who helped bring about the Russian Revolution with him, such as Leon Trotsky, one of the key architects of the Soviet Union. Stalin was so envious and paranoid of his former comrade that he had his henchmen chase Trotsky more than halfway around the globe until they caught up with him in Mexico and stuck an ice pick in his head.

Most of the seven deadly sins aren't normally lethal in the physical sense. But obviously jealousy can and does lead to murder. The police have often said that their least favorite calls (and most dangerous calls) are usually the domestic quarrels. In those contexts, just the right mix of envy and anger can often turn fatal. I should point out, though, that jealousy by no means always leads to murder. In fact, consider these polling results reported by Ralph B. Hupka of California State University, Long Beach: "Surveys have revealed that between 37% and 50% of the respondents report having had extramarital affairs. . . . Yet far less than 0.01% of the U. S. male population commits murder in response to adultery."[4]

Norwegian Legend

There is a Norwegian legend about a little gray mountain bird called *heilo* (pronounced like "halo"). Its song is not a song at all but a sad and haunting cry. The story goes that she used to sing beautifully, while praising God and enjoying His creation. But an old female troll with magical powers, whose name was Black-sick, heard the heilo's beautiful song and became so enraged with jealousy that she stole the little bird's song. In its place, she gave the heilo her own cry. Now, the sky in that part of the country is often gray, and the little gray bird is trapped between bare, gray mountains. The bird's sad cry can thus be heard in the mountain regions

> *The jealous are troublesome to others, but a torment to themselves.*
>
> —William Penn

until the end of time when God will right all wrong, and the little heilo will receive her beautiful song once again.

The troll in this story is nothing less than the personification of envy. Heaven help you if you fall into her clutches. Yet envy isn't so much a wicked witch outside of us, as in this legend, as it is an evil root within us that can grow with the right combination of thoughts, including the thought of *perceived injustice*.

Perceived Injustices

Often it is the people close to us whom we really envy. The siblings, the friends, the coworkers, the people we know (who are roughly at our level). If something great happens to them (but not us), we often feel that it should have been us; and we think, "It's not fair!" Psychologist Richard H. Smith of Boston University comments on the link between envy and perceived injustice. First, he quotes a Pushkin play, the theme of which was dramatized in the movie about Mozart, *Amadeus,* a movie whose plot was built on envy. You will recall that one composer (Salieri) had only mediocre musical talent, but he loved music and he worked hard at it. Meanwhile, another composer (Mozart) was phenomenally blessed with talent but appeared frivolous with it. (Whether this story is entirely true or not, I'll leave up to the historians. Fiction or not, it gives us a good picture of the envious heart.) Pushkin wrote:

> Who dares to say that ever proud Salieri
> Could stoop to envy, like a loathsome snake
> Trampled upon by men, yet still alive
> And impotently gnawing sand and dust?
> No one! . . . But now—myself, I say it—now
> I do know envy. Yes, Salieri envies,
> Deeply, in anguish envies.—O ye Heavens!
> Where, where is justice, when the sacred gift,
> When deathless genius come not to reward
> Perfervid [impassioned] love and utter denial,
> And toils and strivings and beseeching prayers,
> But puts a halo round a lack-wit's skull,
> A frivolous idler's brow? . . . O Mozart, Mozart![5]

In plain English, Salieri was asking this: Where is justice when musical genius is bestowed upon the frivolous Mozart and not me—who passionately loves music, who has worked hard to develop greater skill in music, and who has earnestly prayed to that end? About this quote, Smith wrote, "Salieri's envy is linked to the

---

Probably the greatest harm done by vast wealth is the harm that we of moderate means do ourselves when we let the vices of envy and hatred enter deep into our own nature.

—Theodore Roosevelt

injustice of God's bestowing on the 'frivolous idler' Mozart the sublime musical gifts that he, Salieri, deserves more."[6] This brings up a point that Smith and other psychologists make, and that is that the person who envies often feels *justified* in their resentment. He feels that *he,* not the person he envies, deserves the talent, the glory, the possession, the power, or whatever it is. Smith wrote:

> It is often noted, so much so that it can seem a trivial observation, that envy can masquerade as resentment. . . . That is, another's *legitimate* advantage will be construed by the envying person as *illegitimate,* so that envious feelings come across to oneself and to others as resentment or righteous indignation rather than envy. . . . I argue that the person feeling envy (in its typically hostile form) will believe that the envied person's advantage is to some degree unfair. Hostile feelings are an immediate, natural response to felt injustice, and thus such unfairness beliefs provide an explanation for these feelings.[7]

> *Envious feelings are, at least in part, characterized by a sense of injustice.*
>
> —Peter Salovey,
> *The Psychology of Jealousy & Envy*

It is widely held that "a sense of injustice is usually present in envy."[8] Remember the older brother in the parable of the prodigal son? He resented the feast his father threw for his spendthrift brother, that good-for-nothing who squandered his inheritance. He envied the attention his brother was now receiving. He felt that it wasn't fair. I imagine that Cain felt it unfair that Abel's sacrifice was accepted by God, while his was not.

Envy Among Siblings

As it was with Cain and Abel, so it has been with many other children. What they are envious of is love, affection, and acceptance.

Whether this is perceived or real, it can cause rage, which can lead to violence. What sometimes happens is that a parent can withhold his or her love from one child, and yet lavish it on another one.

The Smothers Brothers sometimes captured this sibling rivalry in a humorous way. One brother complained, "Mom always liked you best. She gave you a dog as a pet and only gave me a chicken!" Then the other brother piped in, "Yeah. But your chicken ate my dog!"

All humor aside, some families are ruled by such rivalry. Look at the seemingly unending rivalry between Jacob and Esau, which began even at birth (Gen. 25–27).

Look at the case of Joseph, Jacob's favorite son. Jacob had twelve sons through his two wives and their maidens. Note that polygamy—which by nature promotes envy—was tolerated in the Old Testament but condemned in the New (Titus 1:6). Jacob was not a model dad. He created a climate of jealousy among his sons. "Now Israel [Jacob] loved Joseph more than any of his other sons, because he had been born to him in his old age; and he made a richly ornamented robe for him. When his brothers saw that their father loved him more than any of them, they hated him and could not speak a kind word to him" (Gen. 37:3–4). Joseph made his brothers even more jealous by telling them about his dreams, in which all of them bowed down to him. (Gen. 37:7–9). His father rebuked him for telling them the dream. Nonetheless, his brothers were so jealous that they plotted to kill him and tell his father he had been killed by a wild animal. His older brother Reuben talked them out of killing Joseph and convinced them to sell him to some traders who were going to Egypt (Gen. 37:12–36).

> *Envy takes the joy, happiness, and contentment out of living.*
>
> —Billy Graham

By God's providence, Joseph eventually became second in command under Pharaoh in Egypt and saved his family from a famine. He also forgave his brothers.

There are several lessons we can glean from the story of Jacob:

1. Don't show favoritism toward one child. As soon as we feel favoritism towards any of our children, we should ask God's forgiveness and quench it immediately.

2. The sin of envy and jealousy can be passed down from one generation to another, so we should be careful to avoid repeating the same mistakes our parents might have made.

3. We should learn to be satisfied with whatever God gives us because envy and jealousy can lead to other sins.

4. If we are victims of envy or jealousy, we should forgive the offenders and trust God because He has a plan for our lives. We can take encouragement from the words Joseph said to his brothers: "You intended to harm me, but God intended it for good" (Gen. 50:20).

Envy Can Sneak Right Up on Us

The same rivalry and jealousy we see in families also takes place in the workplace. If someone else gets the position or promotion that his colleague thought was rightfully his, then ill feelings can arise. And resentment of that person—if not checked and stopped—can easily develop into both bitterness and hatred.

Envy can develop very gradually and sneak up on us without our even realizing what is happening. Let's say I (Kirsti) am in the checkout line in the grocery store, and I flip through a glossy home improvement magazine. I might have been satisfied with my kitchen that morning, but now that I have seen how a kitchen should *really* look, I can't believe I thought ours was OK! So the seed of discontentment has been planted, and I start to desire a new kitchen or maybe even a whole new house. The next time we are over at some friend's house who has a nicer home than we do, I could start to feel jealous, and over time jealousy can change to resentment. Resentment can poison the soul and sour relationships, and resentment can turn into bitterness and bitterness into hatred if we don't root it out right away.

Envy is something that thrives in the dark. But when the light is shown on it, it sometimes withers away. Psychologist Betsy Cohen, author of a book about envy called *The Snow White Syndrome,* says: "We must bring envy 'into the light.' It is a dark and hidden emotion but easily disarmed. When unacknowledged, envy is dangerous. Bring it into the light, use the Word, and it becomes less potent. We must call it by name—envy."[9]

> *One cannot be envious and happy at the same time.*
>
> —Henry Greber

Covetousness, which we find forbidden at the end of the Ten Commandments, is really the only commandment dealing with thoughts about and towards other people. (The first commandment forbids wrong thoughts and attitudes about God.) But covetousness forbids us to want and desire anything belonging to our neighbor. We seldom recognize envy or covetousness for what it is, and we seldom confess it as a sin. As a matter of fact, an elderly Catholic priest once said that in all his years of hearing confessions, he had never once heard a person confessing to the sin of covetousness. In the sixteenth century, St. Francis Xavier made a similar statement.

> I have heard thousands of confessions, but never one of covetousness.

Covetousness is often tied in with discontentment, and discontentment often comes from criticism. When we criticize each other, it breeds discontentment, which leads to a wish for something else, and in this atmosphere we start to covet what someone else has. It can be anything from dissatisfaction with the way we look to a burning resentment toward the person who has what we want and what we think we deserve.

A friend of ours told us an unbelievable story—unbelievable to us because we are close to our parents. But she was the victim of envy by her own mother. Being the only daughter in the family, and having heard her mother complain so much about girls who just run off and get married, she thought when the time came, she would go home for the wedding. Big mistake. Her father had died three years before, and her mother was still grieving his death. She was so jealous, she wouldn't do anything to help, made her daughter cry the day the photographer took her engagement picture, etc. It would not have mattered whom the daughter married, she told her child quite plainly, "You have a man, and I don't." This shocked the daughter to the core because she had always thought of her mother as being a loving person who had her best interests at heart. The daughter hid her pain and somehow got through the wedding, but it was seven years before she went home to see her mom again. Sadly, the marriage eventually ended in divorce. (Was there a link there?)

> *"A mother takes her two daughters shopping for skirts. She chooses two skirts, a red one and a blue one. The mother asks the older sister, 'Which color do you want? Red or blue?' The older sister is certain, 'I don't care. I just want the one she gets.'"*
>
> —George P. Elliott

Jealousy Vs. Envy

The two words *envy* and *jealousy* are similar, yet Webster's does give different meanings: *envy* is to feel discontent at another's good fortune, or to have a longing or desire to have what another person has; *jealousy* is an intolerant rivalry.[10]

The two Hebrew words in the Old Testament that have been translated into "envy" and "jealousy" are *kana* (envy) and *quana*

> *The great enemy of love is jealousy.*
> *When jealousy creeps into the home,*
> *love packs up and gets ready to depart,*
> *for it cannot thrive under the perpetual*
> *tyranny of a jealous spouse.*
>
> —Ernest Groves

(jealousy). Both have the idea of burning or becoming inflamed. But, if you are envious *(kana),* you become inflamed against someone; and if you are jealous *(quana),* you can be inflamed for or against someone, so jealousy has both a positive and a negative meaning.

The Bible speaks a good deal about God being a jealous God. This can be found even in the Ten Commandments (Exod. 20:5). God is jealous, but He is jealous in the positive sense of the word. He was jealous for His children's devotion. Israel's repeated idolatry—which is a theme throughout the Old Testament—was essentially *adultery* toward God. Their idolatry was spiritual adultery.

The negative aspects of envy and jealousy make them not only synonyms, but more importantly, temptations. The reason we fall into the sin of envy and jealousy is because we are selfish and impatient. Instead of being peacemakers, we sometimes stir up strife. Proverbs 23:17 warns,

"Do not let your heart envy sinners,
but always be zealous for the fear of the LORD."

Sometimes we can be envious not only of sinners, but of other Christians as well. We think we deserve what someone has, and we try to figure out how we can beat them out of it. This is not God's way. His way is peaceable. The Bible says love "does not envy" (1 Cor. 13:4).

Over and over again we may find ourselves envious of those who seem to have it "made in the shade." Two psalms deal with envy: Psalm 37 and Psalm 73. Listen to what Asaph the psalmist said in the latter chapter:

> For I envied the arrogant
>> when I saw the prosperity of the wicked.
> They have no struggles;
>> their bodies are healthy and strong.
> They are free from the burdens common to man;
>> they are not plagued by human ills. . . .
> This is what the wicked are like—
>> always carefree, they increase in wealth. . . .
> When I tried to understand all this,
>> it was oppressive to me
> till I entered the sanctuary of God;
>> then I understood their final destiny.
> (Ps. 73:3–5, 12, 16–17).

Everybody's life is hard, and if you really get to know people, they have problems and sorrows you would never have guessed. Furthermore, some godless persons today may seemingly have a great life in complete defiance of their Creator. From a worldly perspective they may seem to be a success. But what does it profit you if you gain the whole world and lose your soul?

Yet he was jealous,
though he did not show it,
For jealousy dislikes
the world to know it.

—Lord Byron

Also, it's important for us to focus on what *we're* called to do and to stop comparing ourselves with other people, which is often a self-defeating habit. Remember when Peter wanted to know what Jesus's plan was for the apostle John, and Jesus essentially told him, "What is that to you? *You* follow me" (John 21:20–22).

So we should strive to stay close to our Lord and concentrate on the task He has given *us* to do. When we are grateful to Him for where He has placed us and what He has given us, envy and jealousy will flee.

We Could Do More for the Kingdom If We Weren't So Envious

Too often within Christendom today everyone is trying to build their own little fiefdom. Remember the televangelist scandals of a decade ago? They were very detrimental to the cause of Christ, and at the root of this ugly soap opera were some of the seven deadly sins, namely pride, greed, and lust, but above all, envy!

Think of all the church splits and conflicts that boil down to envy. Think of all of the infighting in churches that boils down to

> *The world may be obsessed with celebrities, power and influence. But God is still in the business of confounding the wisdom of man. And he most often builds his kingdom through the faithful obedience of ordinary people.*
>
> —Chuck Colson

envy. While I don't buy in to the theory that denominationalism per se is sin, certainly much of the disunity found in the body of Christ today is. I don't buy in to theological agreements that paper over genuine differences in doctrine. Nonetheless, great unity can be achieved in the body of Christ when we look at what we agree upon, rather than focus on that with which we're divided.

Chuck Swindoll once pointed out that President Reagan had this saying on a plaque on his desk: "There is no limit to what a man can do or where he can go if he doesn't mind who gets the credit." In contrast, envy limits itself to that for which we will get the glory. This reminds me of how some actors quibble over who gets top billing in the movie, the TV program, the play. This is envy at work. Too often there is company politics and backbiting to be found in Christian organizations or in churches. This is envy at work. Envy and lust for power (pride). Yet we serve Jesus who said the great-

> *Envy is an open door to bitterness.*
>
> —Eleanor Doan

est among you is the servant. Paul says, "Let us not become conceited, provoking and envying each other" (Gal. 5:26).

Conclusion

I close with the words of the great American psychologist William James who in 1890 candidly wrote of the envy in his own heart:

> I, who for the time have staked my all on being a psychologist, am mortified if others know much more psychology than I. But I am contented to wallow in the grossest ignorance of Greek. My deficiencies there give me no sense of personal humiliations at all. Had I "pretensions" to be a linguist, it would have been just the reverse. So we have the paradox of a man shamed to death because he is only the second pugilist or the second oarsman in the world. That he is able to beat the whole population of the globe minus one is nothing; he has "pitted" himself to beat that one; and as long as he doesn't do that nothing else counts.[11]

And so, as long as we are held in the grip of envy, we will be miserable, despite how many untold blessings we may have in our life. Let's now turn our attention to how to break free from its icy grip.

chapter 8

Charity

---

*Love is the medicine of all moral evil.
By it the world is to be cured of sin.*

—Henry Ward Beecher

The patriarch of a large extended family in an isolated nineteenth-century mountain village was a terror. He ruled with an iron fist and made life miserable for everyone on the large farm. His son had just brought home his new bride. She had a smile on her face and a song in her heart. She was a devout Christian. The patriarch himself went faithfully to church every Sunday and was the biggest contributor to the local church, so he believed himself to be a good Christian too. But he didn't walk the talk. He managed to silence her song but couldn't wipe the smile from her face or the cheerfulness from her voice. She constantly served her father-in-law, and the meaner he got, the kinder she got. He believed her to be after his money or to be desirous of favoritism.

One February night, the father-in-law got seriously ill; he needed professional medical help. But a blizzard was raging outside, and the menfolk were out trying to save the livestock. So the young wife took off to go the five miles to fetch the doctor. She managed to get him, but in the process she herself caught pneumonia. As she lay struggling for her life, the old patriarch bowed his knees

> *Love looks through a telescope;*
> *envy, through a microscope.*
>
> —Anonymous

at her bedside and asked forgiveness from God and his sweet and loving daughter-in-law. The self-sacrificing love of one young woman changed the bitterness and hatred of an old man, and an entire homestead was transformed. Love conquers all, even the hardest of hearts.

The purpose of this chapter is to focus on love or charity, which is the antidote to envy. In fact, in some ways love is the antidote to all the seven deadly sins:

- A heart full of love is humble.
- If you are loving, you are both content and generous (thus quelling greed).
- If you love others, you wish them well, as opposed to being jealous of their success.
- If you are full of love, you don't fly off the handle in a rage.
- If you love (which gives), you are not consumed by lust (which takes).
- For the sake of those you love, you will take care of your body—not unhealthily gorging yourself.
- If you love others, you will work hard. You will not be selfishly lazy.

See how all the vices melt away before charity. Pride and boasting disappear. Envy flees; anger cannot get a foothold. Greed and jealousy cannot coexist with love. Christian love is the antidote to all vice and all sin in our hearts. That is why Jesus said that if you love God and your neighbor you have fulfilled the law. For the whole law of God is summed up in love.

Returning to envy, one cannot have both it and love toward the same thing at the same time. You can harbor ill feelings toward someone (because of jealousy), or you can wish good for them (because of love). But you can't do both simultaneously.

Envy always wants something. Love is the opposite of envy because it wants to give. The love of God gives by nature. Likewise all Christian charity gives. It gives without expecting anything back. But in all human loves, even though they give to a large extent, there is still the expectation of being loved back. This is true between lovers as well as family members and friends. Only pure Christian charity or love is selfless and giving in nature, and thus it stands forever in contrast with self-serving envy, jealousy, and greed.

The Highest Virtue

Of all the Christian virtues love stands like Mt. Everest among the mountains. It shines like the most brilliant diamond among all the precious stones. The love of God has transformed hearts and minds. It has cast down strongholds of evil. Its recreative power has been the marvel of the world.

A "Well-Worn Subject"

Years ago, Francis Schaeffer wrote an excellent, short book called *The Mark of the Christian*. What is the mark of the Christian? How do we know you are a Christian? By your adherence to a few key doctrines—say from the Synod of 1847? Is it by speaking in tongues? Is it that "we don't smoke or chew or go with girls who do"? What is the sign that you are a Christian? I

> *I love mankind.*
> *It's people*
> *I can't stand!*
>
> —Charles Schultz, *Peanuts*

was talking with a friend a few years ago who told me that the church that led her to Christ also gave her the impression that if you're really a Christian, then you wear skirts no shorter than four inches from your knees and that you have flower patterns on your Bible covers. I would trust that that church didn't really believe that; nonetheless, that was the strong impression she got.

On the contrary to following after rules and regulations, the mark of the Christian is love—in particular, love for the brethren, love for our fellow Christians. Jesus said: "A new command I give you: Love one another. As I have loved you, so you must love one another. By this all men will know that you are my disciples, if you love one another" (John 13:34–35).

Love is such a well-worn subject. It's old hat to so many Christians. But it ought not to be. The Bible hasn't changed. It's sad that you could pack a church seminar on the subject of rock music or the end times, yet hardly have anyone show up to hear a seminar on loving one another. You could do a radio show on the occult and have lots of people call in. But talk about love, and I doubt many would call in. I know. I've tried it.

The thing that's so tragic, though, is that while love should be the dominating trait that characterizes us as Christians, that's not necessarily always the reality among professing Christians. Think of all the backbiting, office politics, and gossip that can take place— even in a Christian organization or a church. I can think of people who have left some ministries with a bad taste in their mouths for ministries, or in some cases, even Christianity. That's terrible. We are called to spread the gospel, not to spread the gossip—but sometimes we seem to do a better job at the latter.

I know of one lady who used to work for a Christian organization and was very disturbed by the way people were treated—as if they were only cogs in a wheel. She got a job in a secular setting and confided in me that she was treated better there than by the ministry that used to employ her. She said they value her as a person at the other organization; whereas they didn't at the ministry. (In other words, the secular business was more *Christian* in how they treated her, while the ministry was more worldly.) She told me that she'll never work for another ministry again. Now that may be a little extreme, but it shows how we have a responsibility to reflect Christian love—especially in an outreach that claims to exist for the purpose of showing Christian love.

"By this will all men know that you are my disciples—that you love one another" (John 13:35). It is by the love we show to our fellow Christians that we give evidence that we belong to Christ. People are seeking love. Real love. And if we know Christ, we can give it.

An interesting strategy of the cults is known as "love bombing." When a new potential convert comes in, they'll "bomb" this person

---

Love—the antidote to envy:

To love anyone is nothing else than to wish that person good.
—St. Thomas Aquinas

In jealousy there is more self-love than love.
—Francois de La Rochefoucauld

Where love is, there is no lack.
—Richard Brome

---

with a great deal of love and attention. They'll go out of their ways to make them feel loved and welcome, until they get them hooked, and then to quote Jesus in a different context, they'll make them twice a son of hell as they are. That's tragic, but it is good strategy. It's a twisted version of Christian love—using love, manipulating people—for a desired end. That's not how Christ loves us.

Christ calls us to love each other *as He loved us.* That's a high calling.

Love in the Early Church

In the early church, Christian love was remarkable. It made history. It helped shape history. By their love, the early Church was able to provide a remarkable witness to the watching world. That's helpful to remember the next time we're tempted to engage in some type of backbiting or gossip. By their love, the early Church was able to provide a shining witness to the watching world.

> *These Christians love each other even before they are acquainted.*
>
> —St. Celsus

Christian charity was new. It was an *innovation*. Charity—organized charity—virtually did not exist in the ancient world.

The eminent historian Will Durant wrote about ancient Rome, which was the most important civilization in antiquity:

> Charity found little scope in this frugal life. Hospitality survived as a mutual convenience at a time when inns were poor and far between; but the sympathetic Polybius reports that "in Rome no one ever gives away anything to anyone if he can help it"—doubtless an exaggeration.[1]

But Christ came and loved us and told us to go and do likewise. It was He who initiated the Good Samaritan ethic (Luke 10). Jesus showed us how love acts in Matthew 25:35-36. And through two thousand years of church history this passage has always been the manual for Christian charity: "I was hungry and you gave me something to eat, I was thirsty and you gave me something to drink, I was a stranger and you invited me in, I needed clothes and you clothed me, I was sick and you looked after me, I was in prison and you came to visit me." When Jesus explained that whatever we do and whatever kindness we show is actually as if we did it for the Lord himself, then orphanages and hospitals became possible for the first time ever. First this shows how totally Christ identifies with our humanity in our suffering, and secondly it shows us how every time we help and care for someone, He takes it as a deed done for Him personally. Even a glass of water given in Christ's name to a thirsty person is an act of worship. Thus it benefits the recipient as well as the giver. In this way it will not be necessary to wish anything in return, because the deed is done for the Lord and that is a reward in and of itself. When this radical teaching was *put into practice,* the early Church turned the world upside down.

The witness of the early Church was profound in terms of their love for one another. Oxford scholar Robin Lane Fox wrote,

> The Christian community stressed the support of its widows, orphans, sick, and disabled, and of those who because of their faith were thrown out of employment or were imprisoned. It ransomed men who were put to servile labour for their faith. It entertained travelers. One church would send aid to another church whose members were suffering from famine or persecution. In theory and to no small degree in practice, the Christian community was a brotherhood, bound together in love, in which reciprocal material help was the rule.[2]

All of this was radical in its time. (It would be radical in our time too.) We may think of it as commonplace, but it was profoundly different from what the world had seen up to this time.

Tertullian (c. 160–c. 215 A.D.) tells us that when the Christians were brought to die in the arena, the crowds would shout, "Look how these Christians love one another."[3] By their love, the early Church prevailed over the Roman Empire, the strongest nation in world history. As Will Durant put it, "Caesar and Christ had met in the arena, and Christ had won."[4] Love conquers all.

Now let's bring this to an individual level: In whose heart would you expect to find envy or love: that of Mother Teresa or

> *To be loved, love.*
>
> —Decimus Magnus Ausonius, *Epigrams*

that of the latest Hollywood star? Which person would be more happy? Yet which one has been "successful" by the world's standard?

But outward works of charity per se don't necessarily squelch envy. Let's suppose for the sake of argument that there are two officers in the Salvation Army competing for the same post. They both may abound in good works. Let's say one is motivated by sincere love; the other out of envy and pride. Even if the latter gets the higher position, who is happier? Who has God's blessings on his life, even if he has the lower position? Who will fare better on Judgment Day? Outward acts of love alone are no guarantee against the inner poison of envy.

> *Amor Vincit Omnia (Love conquers all)*
>
> —Latin expression

Sometimes charity, like anything, can be done with the wrong motives. It can be done to make the worker of charity feel good, as opposed to being done with the recipient's best interests at heart. It can also be done to make the recipient feel inferior and in need of charity. In contrast with this sort of tainted love is God's unconditional love, which gives with no strings attached.

The Love of God—The Source of Our Charity

Ultimately, our love is inspired most by the love of God. What kind of love does God have for us? It is a love that gives. Charity is the love of God among men. It is the self-sacrificing love that drove Jesus from heaven down to earth and all the way to the cross. It is the love that gives without asking anything in return.

What is love? The Bible answers that: "God is love" (1 John 4:8). He is not only the source of true love; He *is* love. John, who explained this, called himself "the disciple whom Jesus loved." He wrote, "This is love: not that we loved God, but that he loved us and sent his Son as an atoning sacrifice for our sins" (1 John 4:10).

How do we become more loving? Since God is the source, we have to draw close to Him. It is by meditating on His love for us and glimpsing what He has done on our behalf (for example, Christ's suffering for us, in our place, for our redemption) that we start to love Him. "We love because he first loved us" (1 John 4:19).

Disunity in the Body of Christ

Too often because of envying and pride, we create petty divisions in the body of Christ. We split over trivial matters. We divide over nonessentials. For example, churches have literally split over the carpeting of the sanctuary! (The real issue in such a case is power—and thus, pride.) People even leave the church forever over such needless controversies. In cases like this, the mark of a Christian—love—is usurped by the mark of Cain's sin—envy.

The fact that there are 23,500 denominations points to the sad state of our Christian ministry.[5] Granted, some doctrinal fights are worth fighting, e.g., over basics (like the virgin birth or the resurrection of Christ), but other times, church fights simply boil down to conflicts over pride, envy, and anger. We need a lot less envying and a lot more charity in the body of Christ today.

> *Love is more than a characteristic of God; it is His character.*
>
> —Anonymous

On the positive side, in *Born Again,* Chuck Colson told how amazed he was to discover the unity in Christian fellowship that transcended the bounds of political views and affiliations. As a new Christian in the early 1970s, Nixon's former hatchet man was amazed to pray with and to genuinely love and be loved by the liberal Democratic Senator Howard Hughes or the liberal Republican Senator Mark Hatfield. It was a revelation to him to experience fellowship with former political enemies.

I find that among those who are truly regenerate—despite their denomination—there is often a working unity. I experience it all the time in my job working in Christian communications. I interview people of various denominations for Dr. Kennedy's television ministry. We don't get into nuances of credal differences (not that those things are not necessarily important), but we focus on things we do agree upon and we focus on today's issues of importance to Christians of all stripes. I've heard a great statement sometimes attributed to St. Augustine and sometimes to Blaise Pascal. In any event, it stands on its own:

In essential things, unity.

In nonessentials, liberty.

In all things, charity.

Amen!

So How Do We Cultivate Love?

If it's not in our nature to love, how do we come to do it? First of all, love is a commitment, not a feeling. Feelings come and feelings go. But the commitment to love remains. Hollywood marriages are often built on the sand because they're based on the false notion that love is merely a feeling. In contrast, a Christian marriage is built on the solid foundation of a commitment first to Christ and then to each other.

> *Christian love, either towards God or towards man, is an affair of the will.*
>
> —C. S. Lewis,
> *Mere Christianity*

So how do we cultivate love rather than envy? If envy is truly the first thought that comes to the heart when you see others doing well (but not you), then ask God to make you truly *thankful* for that person's success. For example, suppose you're a minister who is tempted to envy another pastor whose ministry is growing faster. Instead of stewing in jealousy, breathe a prayer—of thanksgiving—for the brother whose ministry is doing so well. After all, if his is a Christ-centered church, then the kingdom of God is advancing.

Look for the good in other people's successes. If you can't sincerely wish them well in your own strength, then ask God to enable you to do it.

This is easier said than done. But we know that envy is like spiritual cancer, whereas love is live-giving.

If you're an entrepreneur, and you envy the success of others in your field who are doing better, the same principle applies—if they're Christians. If they're not saved and if they never come to Christ, then who could *possibly* envy them on Judgment Day and thereafter?!? To envy today's most successful non-Christians makes no sense in the light of eternity. And to envy a successful Christian brother reflects love of self, rather than love of God. It is most surely a sin from which to repent. If you ever have this tendency, ask the Lord for a heart full of love, and consciously force yourself to thank the Lord for his success.

Suppose you are in an office setting, and you envy the quicker advancement of those around you. Again, it's easy for the monster of envy to rear its ugly head. But thanking God for that person from your heart and asking Him for help to love them can help ward off envy. If you've been unjustly left behind in a promotion, there may be opportunities to state your case. If you're ultimately treated wrongly and it's time to move on, you're much better off forgiving and forgetting than you are letting a root of bitterness grow in your heart. When you let envy fester in your heart, then the person you envy (or the person you blame for the promotion you were denied) controls you. You give them even more power than they would have normally.

> *Love cures people—both the ones who give it and the ones who receive it.*
>
> —Karl Menninger

Replacing Evil with Good

In short, let good thoughts and practices replace evil ones. Let thankfulness replace resentment. Let charity replace envy. We need to train ourselves to replace bad thoughts with good thoughts.

How do we do this practically? Paul gives us a lesson in putting off the old self and putting on the new self in the letter to the Ephesians, chapters four and five. The new self is created by God and nurtured in the "attitude of your minds" (Eph. 4:23). Thankfulness is a key to transforming the mind from envy and bitterness to love.

Paul tells us to exchange the old for the new. For example, instead of stealing, do something useful so that you "may have something to share with those in need" (4:28). That way greed and envy are replaced by generosity. Instead of unwholesome talk, at the moment you want to say something inappropriate, replace it with that which is "helpful for building others up according to their needs, that it may benefit those who listen" (4:29).

Next Paul shows us how to get rid of bitterness, rage, anger, slander, and all malice. Substitute them with kindness and compassion for one another. Let bitterness melt away by "forgiving each other, just as in Christ God forgave you" (4:32). The key here is God's forgiveness to us. When we think of what we have been forgiven for, then it is easier to forgive and to be kind and compassionate to others.

Paul continues by urging us to have nothing to do with the fruitless works of darkness, but rather we should "live as children of light (for the fruit of the light consists in all goodness, righteousness and truth)" (5:8–9). Instead of being drunk with wine, we should be filled with the Holy Spirit, and one way to do that is by singing "psalms, hymns and spiritual songs . . . in your heart to the Lord" (5:19). Every negative thought has a positive counterpart, just as every vice has its opposite virtue. And as children of the light, we can train ourselves to counter sinful thoughts with godly thoughts, hurtful words with healing ones, and sinful acts with positive deeds. It all starts in the mind and the renewing of our minds through the Word of God, memorizing and meditating on it day and night.

The Example of Hannah

Another way envy can be thwarted is to look to the provision of God for help in your situation. If you feel envious toward another, ask Him to change your heart *and* to change your situation if necessary. For example, Hannah, the mother of Samuel, was barren. Meanwhile, her husband's other wife (polygamy brings nothing but heartache) taunted her all the time, for the other woman was fertile. Hannah felt nothing but grief and shame for bearing no children. But she prayed fervently at the temple, so much so that Eli the priest thought she was drunk. When he understood her heart's desire, he promised her that within a year she would have a child, which is what happened. The source of any potential envy in Hannah's heart was stopped at the root.

Conclusion

Love is the greatest way to thwart the deadly sin of envy. But love is easier said than done. One of the keys to cultivating love in our hearts toward our fellowman is by cultivating love for God in our hearts. One of the best ways of doing that is by contemplating what Jesus has done for us on the cross. When we meditate on that, it can melt even the coldest heart. The ground is level at the foot of the cross. There is no room for any kind of jealousy or brother-hating at the foot of the cross. Nothing can reduce envy like cultivating Christian love and charity. "And now these three remain: faith, hope and love. But the greatest of these is love" (1 Cor. 13:13).

chapter 9

Anger

Whatever is begun in anger
ends in shame.

—Ben Franklin

Monday, October 26, 1987, Miami, Florida. The stock market had collapsed one week earlier, with the Dow plunging a record 504 points. Yes, it was true that some investors had suffered heavy losses—there had been serious margin calls—but all had been fairly quiet in the suburban, tree-shaded office of Merrill Lynch.

Arthur Kane, 53, a nonpracticing attorney and longtime investor who made his living by playing the market, seemed to be his usually composed self. He had been coming to the Merrill Lynch office on a daily basis for years to watch the stock ticker display on the second floor and to consult with his broker, Lloyd Kolokoff. So there was little warning for what was about to happen.

Suddenly, at 11:14 A.M.—Bang! Bang! Bang! Shots rang out in the southeast corner of the second floor. The branch manager's office was located there! Terrified sales assistants and clients

> *We are a violent people with a violent history.*
> *The instinct for violence has seeped into the*
> *bloodstream of our national life.*
>
> —Arthur Schlesinger

scurried to take cover or crowd down the fire escape. Kane had shot the branch manager, Jose F. Argilagos in the face, killing him instantly, shot his broker in the spine, paralyzing him for life, and then killed himself.

The broker's desk and the branch manager's office were located in opposite corners of the second floor. Kane's revenge was so calculated that he had purchased a gun at the gun shop across the street the day before, hidden it in his briefcase, and calmly convinced his broker to take him to the branch manager's office so he could shoot both of them at once. Henry Simmons, a stockbroker who had retired from the Miami Merrill Lynch office the year before, told the press, "It's unbelievable that the man would ask his broker to go into the officer of the manager and then kill them. He apparently considered his broker and the manager responsible."[1] This is just one of many instances in our time when people can't control their anger. Because of unchecked anger, there are now some dangerous places in America . . .

- The workplace
- Public school campuses
- The highway (with the rising cases of road rage)

In this chapter we're going to explore the issue of the deadly sin of anger.

Anger—Not a New Problem

He hid the dead body in the sand. He was sure that no one had seen the murder he had committed. "Anyway," he reasoned, "the man deserved to die. No Egyptian taskmaster has a right to

> *Temper is dangerous. Medically.*
> *Dr. Willard Harris of Ohio State University reports that anger and fear affect the heart in identical ways: the pulse speeds up and the breathing rate doubles.*
>
> *Dr. John Henderson writes, 'acute anger has been associated with an acute heart attack. Heart damage can be done by repeated bouts of anger over a long period of time.'*
>
> *But more serious is the sickness a hair-trigger temper produces in a man's personality. It prevents personal and social development, halts all spiritual progress, cuts him off from fellow humans, and blocks all good judgement.*
>
> *Temper is a sign of weakness, not strength.*
>
> —David Augsburger, *The Freedom of Forgiving*

beat a Hebrew slave that way. I did it. And no one is the wiser." But the following day, when Moses was trying to settle a fight between two Hebrews, he found out that he had been watched. The aggressor said to him sarcastically, "Who made you ruler and judge over us? Are you thinking of killing me as you killed the Egyptian?" (Exod. 2:14). Moses had to leave the country fast. He went to the wilderness before the Pharaoh could catch and kill him, and he lived there forty years until the Pharaoh died.

Moses killed the Egyptian because he was angry. Question: Is it wrong to get angry? Here is what one modern expert on anger said:

> Anger is a signal, and one worth listening to. Our anger may be a message that we are being hurt, that our rights are being violated, that our needs or wants are not being adequately met, or simply that something is not right. Our anger may tell us that we are not addressing important emotional issues in our lives, or that too much of our self—our beliefs, values, desires or ambitions—is being compromised in a relationship. Our anger may be a signal that we are doing more than we can comfortably do or give. Or our anger may warn us that others are doing too much for us, at the expense of our own competence and growth. Just as physical pain tells us to take our hand off the hot stove, the pain of our anger preserves the very integrity of our self.[2]

> *I once slapped a Christian's face during a conversation we had. He got me mad. I had anger in me and I slapped him. When I did, he turned the other cheek. I had not courage to slap again. I was stunned.*
>
> —Letter from a Canadian friend to John Augsburger

Question: How does this expert's opinion line up with what the Bible says about anger? The Bible has a good deal of advice to give about handling anger, but nowhere does it forbid us to get angry. Indeed, God made us in His image. In addition to being a God of love, He is also a God of wrath. The purpose of God's anger is to get everyone to recognize that He alone is holy and to worship Him with a pure heart. He is offended when people do not. Those who refuse, He destroys; those who forget, He chastises so they will repent and return. God's anger is not petty, nor whimsically vindictive, but always in keeping with his eternal plan. Over and over again in the Old Testament, God became angry with His people, especially when they turned to other gods or when they forgot His mercy and His help in the past. The purpose of God's anger is to bring His children back into a right relationship with Him.

Righteous Anger

When Jesus came to earth, He also became angry. He got angry when He saw what people were doing to the temple, and He cleansed it, not just once, but twice. The first time was at the first Passover just after His baptism (John 2:13–16). The second time was near the end of His ministry (Matt. 21:12–13; Mark 11:15–17). Let's look at how John described the first cleansing:

> When it was almost time for the Jewish Passover, Jesus went up to Jerusalem. In the temple courts he found men selling cattle, sheep and doves, and others sitting at tables exchanging money. So he made a whip out of cords, and drove all from the temple area, both sheep and cattle; he scattered the coins of the money changers and overturned their tables. To those who sold doves he said, "Get these out of here! How dare you turn my Father's house into a market!"

Jesus was angry because the court of the temple was supposed to be a place of worship for the Gentile believers. It was called the Court of the Gentiles. But now, merchants were selling oxen and sheep and doves for sacrifice and for common use. He did not complain to the chief priests because He knew they were allowing it and charging rent for the space. As for the money changers, all the money given to the temple had to be in Tyrian silver coin.[3] Every Israelite twenty years or older was required to pay an annual tax of a half shekel. The amount was the same for the rich and the poor (Exod. 30:11–16). Jesus was angry because the money changers were charging exorbitant rates.

The second time Jesus cleansed the temple, His condemnation was even stronger. The first time He said they had made the temple a marketplace; the second time He said, "Is it not written 'My house will be called a house of prayer for all nations'? But you have made it a 'den of robbers'" (Mark 11:17). Note that both times when He cleansed the temple, no one tried to stop Him. They knew He was doing the right thing. By cleansing the temple, Jesus fulfilled the prophesy of Malachi 3:1–3 that He would purify the sons of Levi, and lay claim to Messiahship. Also, the words from Psalm 69:9 were fulfilled: "For zeal for your house consumes me."

> *A tart temper never mellows with age, and a sharp tongue is the only edged tool that grows keener with constant use.*
>
> —Washington Irving

Angry Feelings Toward God?

The Bible and especially the psalms are honest about our feelings towards God, but God's Word warns us against being angry with God: "Woe to him who quarrels with his Maker" (Isa. 45:9a). When Job was angry with God, the Lord answered, "Would you discredit my justice? Would you condemn me to justify yourself?" (Job 40:8) The danger is not in feeling mad; the sin is when we believe God to be unjust and tell Him that He is wrong and we are right. In our anger towards God, we distrust His goodness and doubt His love for us. That is wrong.

When it comes to our relationships with each other, the Bible has much to say regarding anger:

- "Refrain from anger and turn from wrath; do not fret—it leads only to evil" (Ps. 37:8).
- "A gentle answer turns away wrath, but a harsh word stirs up anger" (Prov. 15:1).

- "Do not make friends with a hot-tempered man, / do not associate with one easily angered, / or you may learn his ways and get yourself ensnared" (Prov. 22:24–25).
- "A man who controls his temper [is better] than one who takes a city" (Prov. 16:32).
- "Do not be quickly provoked in your spirit, / for anger resides in the lap of fools" (Eccles. 7:9).
- "But I tell you that anyone who is angry with his brother will be subject to judgment" (Matt. 5:22).
- "And you, fathers, do not provoke your children to wrath, but bring them up in the training and admonition of the Lord" (Eph. 6:4, NKJV).
- "Everyone should be quick to listen, slow to speak and slow to become angry, for man's anger does not bring about the righteous life that God desires" (James 1:19).

The key advice on anger is found in the Old Testament and repeated in the New:

- "Be angry, and do not sin. Meditate within your heart on your bed, and be still" (Ps. 4:4, NKJV).

The New Testament points out that if we sin in our anger, we then give the devil a foothold in our lives (Eph. 4:27). If everybody would obey this verse and *never* go to bed angry with another person, our marriages would stay intact, our family life would be pleasant, our workplaces would be much nicer, our schools would be safer, and our churches would not have so much friction and so many power struggles. In short, if we only could get rid of our anger right away, we would basically live together in peace.

Defining Anger and Its Corollaries

What is meant by anger? Anger comes in various types and degrees of emotional intensity, such as rage, fury, indignation, and wrath. Here is how Webster differentiates them:[4]

- *Anger,* the broadest term, implies emotional agitation of no specified intensity, aroused by great displeasure.

- *Rage* suggests a violent outburst of anger in which self-control is lost.
- *Fury* is an overwhelming rage of a frenzied kind that borders on madness.
- *Indignation* is righteous anger aroused by what is considered unjust, mean, or shameful.
- *Wrath* is a deep indignation, expressing itself in the desire to punish or get revenge.

The Bible uses two of these words, *anger* and *wrath*. God is allowed to be vengeful, but we are not. In Romans 12:19, we read: "Do not take revenge, my friends, but leave room for God's wrath, for it is written: 'It is mine to avenge; I will repay,' says the Lord."

> *Resentment is suicide.*
>
> —Alcoholics Anonymous

If anger is a signal that something needs correcting, and we are not allowed to take revenge, what are we supposed to do? How can we be angry and not sin? What should Moses have done?

> *Do you know the origin of the word resentment? It comes from the Latin word* resento, *which essentially means to re-feel. Someone may hurt you deeply. Temporarily, you may shove that tragic experience into your subconscious. But then something happens to conjure up that painful memory. And you re-feel the full agony and hurt of it. You may even externalize those feelings by lashing out in anger and resentment at someone else.*
>
> —Dr. Paul Faulkner

Today we live in a culture in which many people, for various reasons, have decided not to show any anger at all. I have a friend who says, "I never get angry because when I do, it just destroys me." Or, to put it in a lighter way: A man was working in the credit department of a jewelry store when an irate customer replied to a payment reminder with this line, "I get so think that I can't mad straight."[5] Will Rogers warned, "People who fly into a rage always make a bad landing."[6] Publicus Syrus said, "An angry man is angry with himself when he returns to reason."[7]

Consequences of Anger

Getting angry also produces unpleasant physical effects. The obvious signs are a red face, swollen neck veins, stumbling for words, and even blurred vision because anger clouds the visual centers of the brain. Dr. Walter Cannon of Harvard University describes the symptoms more precisely:

> Respiration deepens; the heart beats more rapidly; the arterial pressure rises; the blood is shifted from the stomach and intestines to the heart, central nervous system, and the muscles; the processes of the alimentary canal cease; sugar is freed from the reserves in the liver; the spleen contracts and discharges its contents of concentrated corpuscles, and adrenaline is secreted.[8]

Did you know that expressing anger can make you a potential candidate for a stroke? A recent study of more than two thousand men, mostly in their fifties, found that those who had uncontrolled anger were *twice as likely* to have a stroke as opposed to those who were "able to defuse their anger."[9] Dr. Susan Everson of the University of Michigan School of Medicine conducted the study and released its findings at the 1997 convention of the American Heart Association. She spells out the moral of the story: "The message of the study is not to suppress anger. What people need to do is try and manage their anger and don't let it get to explosive levels or identify the things that make you angry."[10]

In our time we've seen angry children blow away their compatriots. This growing phenomenon has stunned the nation. And in many cases it stems back to the inability of these young people to handle the rage inside of them. One of these children involved in a public school shooting in the bloody school year of 1997–1998 was an eleven-year-old from Arkansas, who, along with his thirteen-year-old cousin, allegedly shot some students and a teacher. The sheriff reported that one day the child was shooting a rifle at fellow classmates; the next night, he was curling up in the jail and crying for his mother. It's incredible that these things are happening. The deadly sin of anger continues to add to the death toll.

Of all the deadly sins, I would think that more deaths are caused by this sin than any other. As I said earlier, police routinely say that the one type of dispute they dread more than any other is the family feud, where they are called upon to keep the peace in a domestic quarrel. Often these domestic fights end with a killing because one of the spouses (usually the husband) couldn't control his temper.

Several decades ago, Dale Carnegie wrote of a sixty-eight-year-old cafe owner in Spokane, Washington, who died because of anger. He died "by flying into a rage because his cook insisted on drinking coffee out of a saucer. He was so indignant that he grabbed a revolver and started to chase the cook and fell dead from heart failure—with his hand still gripping the gun. The coroner's report declared that anger had caused the heart failure."[11] One time an acquaintance told me he had just witnessed a death that very morning caused by anger. Some man was complaining at a city council meeting about a slight increase in taxes, and he dropped dead in his anger. Like several of the seven deadly sins, anger can kill—not only the one who is angry but also the object of his rage.

Road Rage

An unbelievable phenomenon in our time involving anger is "road rage," in which a total stranger literally shoots another stranger because he cuts him off or angers him in some other way. Consider these ludicrous but true cases of the past few years:

- A family of three supposedly cut off a driver who then pulled out a gun and got alongside and shot at the offending car, killing the wife. This took place on Christmas day, no less.[12]
- Two cars of hoodlums drove along either side of another car. They began harassing this car of total strangers. When its driver tried to pull over and get away, one of the hoodlums shot at them and ended up killing their infant son.[13]
- A teacher supposedly cut off a total stranger in traffic. The stranger motioned him to pull over. As they exchanged a few harsh words, the stranger fatally shot the teacher.[14]

Tragically, this phenomenon is on the rise. *Unsolved Mysteries* reported that in the last several years, incidents of road rage have been increasing by 7 percent a year.[15] It is the deadly sin of anger brought into a new arena.

Ways People Handle Their Anger

For a variety of reasons, people may know they are angry and decide to stuff it, or they may be in complete denial and stuff it. Denial of anger has many causes: as a child they were not allowed to show negative emotions; it does not fit with the image they have of themselves, such as "I am a jolly person" or "I am a calm person"; they are afraid it might drastically change their job situation, marital status, or lifestyle so they prefer not to "rock the boat."

Dr. Theodore Isaac Rubin is an expert who believes the "stuffers" are wrong. He believes that anger needs to be expressed. In his *The Angry Book,* he explains that unexpressed anger is like a poison because when we don't express it directly, it takes unhealthy forms. He spends a good many chapters on detailing these poisons, so that we can recognize them. Some of the poisons he includes are these: worry, depression, guilt, overeating, self-imposed starvation, not being able to sleep, sleeping too much, overworking, overexercising, compulsions, phobias, illnesses, imagined illnesses. Then he encourages us to take a chance on anger. Dr. Rubin wrote:

> Anger doesn't kill. This seems obvious, but it isn't to many people; anger doesn't kill healthy relationships and it certainly does not kill people. If anything, denied anger, perverting and twisting, results in the killing of relationships, and people, too. . . . Feeling angry and exchanging angry feelings strengthens true love, and are actually life affirming.[16]

In the opposing camp, opposite the "stuffers," we have the "blasters." Blasters believe it is their constitutional right to be openly angry, and they are angry often. They use anger as a weapon. They let you know, "If I can't have what I want, I'm going to scream, throw things, make a scene in public, etc." Their explosions are so unpleasant that others give in to them. Because they get whatever they want by being angry, anger becomes a habit, a way of life. The main weapon of this group is the tongue. James 3 tells us

> *He is a fool who cannot get angry, but he is a wise man who will not.*
>
> —Seneca

how much damage the tongue can do: "Consider what a great forest is set on fire by a small spark. The tongue also is a fire. . . . It is a restless evil, full of deadly poison" (James 3:5b–6a, 8b).

The blasters we have just described are selfish people, and they know it. But there is another category of blasters who consider themselves to be unselfish. They get angry on behalf of other people. When they see someone being mistreated in a mean, unjust, or shameful way, it arouses their righteous indignation. They believe they have a right to be angry, and many times they do. Their problem is that they go overboard. When does blasting, which they use to call attention to an injustice, turn into vengeance? And is blasting the best way to get results? How should they call attention to the evil of abortion? Some people might write a letter to the editor. Others might picket an abortion clinic. There have even been some radical people who have killed an abortionist. But two wrongs do not make a right. Vengeance belongs to God (Rom. 12:19). And "man's anger does not bring about the righteous life that God desires" (James 1:20). When we realize this truth, it brings us peace and relief. Because if we truly believe that God is just, and that all wrongs shall be put right by Him, we do not need to worry anymore about orchestrating our own justice. God will take care of it. Now, of course, this doesn't mean we shouldn't do all we humanly can to make things right. But it means to leave the results up to Him. Meanwhile, God hasn't called us to be little Rambos in the church, making every wrong right.

In between the groups of the stuffers and the blasters are the "loose cannons." They know they are angry but misdirect their anger at someone less threatening. For example, if they are angry with their boss, they criticize the spouse or scold the children. To vent their anger, they often bring up controversial issues and bait their victim into arguing with them.

Then we have "the smolderers." They may or may not express their anger; they may talk about it to whomever wants to listen, but they cannot get rid of it. They keep their anger burning for years. For example, someone who is eighty years old could still be angry at their parents who died long ago. Many people hang on to their anger; they will not forgive and forget. They hurt themselves, because they set up a negative emotional charge between themselves and the person with whom they are angry and unconsciously can take on that person's negative characteristics. If the person was a verbally abusive alcoholic, they may become the same.

To summarize, we are tempted to misuse anger in several ways:

- To stuff it, knowingly or unknowingly.
- To use it as a weapon, selfishly or unselfishly.
- To misdirect it towards someone less threatening.
- To keep it burning for years like a smoldering fire.

Keeping Anger in Check

We can handle anger without sinning if we follow five principles.

1. *Count to ten.* Don't strike while the iron is hot. In Ecclesiastics 7:9 we read, "Do not be quickly provoked in your spirit, for anger resides in the lap of fools." Distance yourself until you have time to collect your thoughts. Moses' quick action cost him forty years of exile.

2. *Speak directly to the person with whom you are angry.* Matthew 5:23–24 says, "Therefore if you are offering your gift at the altar and there remember that your brother has something against you, leave your gift there in front of the altar. First go and be reconciled to your brother; then come and offer your gift." Speaking directly takes a lot of courage. When we avoid doing it, we often misdirect our anger at someone else, or end up gossiping. Is there someone in your life whom you need to confront? It's scary but well worth the effort.

3. *State exactly what you want.* Do not be vague; do not beat around the bush. Be firm but polite. Do not put the other person down by using any of these substitutes: analyzing, blaming, diagnosing, interpreting, interrogating, labeling, lecturing, moralizing, ordering, preaching, ridiculing, warning, buttonholing.

> *He who can suppress a moment's anger may prevent a day of sorrow.*
>
> —Tryon Edwards

Use "I" messages instead of "you" messages. Not: "Why are you home so late? You're always late." Instead: "I felt so scared when you got home late because I thought maybe you had been in an accident." Think and pray about what you are going to say. Moses told Pharaoh straight out, "Let my people go!" (Exod. 5:1).

4. *Expect resistance and be persistent.* It took Moses ten tries before the Pharaoh finally agreed to let the Israelites go. When Moses killed the Egyptian taskmaster, he was taking a hit-and-run

approach, and that is why he did not succeed; but when he was firmly persistent with Pharaoh, he freed himself and all his people.

5. *"Do not let the sun go down on your wrath."* This vital principle means we should try to resolve issues as quickly as possible. It means we should forgive and forget. Recently, we heard of the tragic murder-suicide of comedian Phil Hartman and his wife. His attorney said that the couple "had a pattern of arguing at night, and he would go to sleep and everything would be OK in the morning."[17] Not good. This is a classic example of "letting the sun go down on your anger."

> *It is he who is in the wrong who first gets angry.*
>
> —William Penn

Conclusion

There was once a young man who got good grades at school, but his teachers warned that he "needed to learn to control his violent temper. Friends remember that the boy generally avoided confrontations, but when provoked, he could explode with frightening ferocity."[18] That young man was Ted Bundy. Granted, that's an extreme example. Nonetheless, it's a sober warning to make sure that we keep the deadly sin of anger in check.

chapter 10

Forgiveness

Before we get to feeling too smug, let's be honest enough to admit there's a little Pharisee in all of us. Harmful though it is, we find a lot of security in our iron bars and solid walls. You and I could list at least ten 'spiritual locks' that hold us prisoner . . . one such spiritual lock would certainly be "I cannot forgive."

—Chuck Swindoll

The hour was dark, and the birds had stopped their singing. The sun had blackened even though it was in the middle of the day. And the Son of God was dying a cruel and vicious death. With parched lips barely able to form words, He uttered an astounding prayer. A prayer that has actually caused many a person to become one of His followers. He said: "Father, forgive them for they know not what they do." Here Jesus forgave and asked His Father to forgive those responsible for putting Him to death. And yet we can't seem to forgive people if they look at us cross-eyed.

Sometimes people say: "I'll forgive you, but I won't forget it." What they don't realize is that to forgive is to pledge to forget. I can think of a situation early in our marriage, where I claimed to have forgiven my wife for a wrong committed. She had apologized, and we had made up. But later, whenever we'd be fighting, I'd bring up this particular episode. This was very bad on my part because it showed I hadn't really forgiven her in the first place. When I realized that, I stopped bringing it up; and I stopped remembering it. When we continually relive and replay in our minds the sins that others have committed against us, then that undermines our forgiveness.

> *People who fight fire with fire usually end up with ashes.*
>
> —Dear Abby

Jesus forgave His executors from the cross, Stephen asked God to forgive his cruel murderers, Corrie ten Boom forgave her Nazi captors in a concentration camp, and American POW Jacob DeShazer forgave his cruel Japanese captors during World War II, but some people can't even forgive their spouses for squeezing the toothpaste tube the wrong way. How we need forgiveness in our day, when divorce ravages so many marriages, when our courts are clogged, when violent acts of anger are often committed on our streets.

The Example of Stephen

Their hate could not touch him. Summoned before the Sanhedrin to make what would be his last defense, Stephen's face shone like the face of an angel (Acts 6:15). Reviewing Israel's history, he explained eloquently how Moses and the tabernacle had been but instruments of God, and how Christ had now superseded them. They didn't want to hear how this made them murderers. It cut them in two. They gnashed their teeth in torment. When he continued, radiantly looking up into heaven, to describe a vision he was having at that very moment, of Jesus standing on the right hand of God, they screamed, stopped their ears, and took him outside the city to stone him. Before he died, Stephen called on God, saying, "'Lord Jesus, receive my spirit.' Then he fell on his knees and cried out, 'Lord, do not hold this sin against them'"

(Acts 7:59–60). Thus, Stephen became the first Christian martyr, in his death following the example of Jesus and setting an example of ultimate forgiveness for all those that would follow him.

How was Stephen able to forgive? All of his rights had been violated.

All of us have been hurt by others; all of us need to forgive. When we are deeply wounded, trounced on, ripped off, betrayed, the test comes: can we forgive? Do you have a hurt that just won't go away? You may very well know for your own mental health that you should let it go, but somehow you can't. You can't forgive and you can't forget.

What makes us hang on to anger? It is the idea that we have been wronged, and that justice has not been served. The more we think about it, the worse it gets. We can't change what happened, but we will change ourselves by holding on to it. Every time we think about it, we get angry all over again. Our compulsive rethinking serves to dig a rut that gets deeper with each round.

> *Forgiveness does not leave the hatchet handle sticking out of the ground.*
>
> —Anonymous

Why Should We Forgive?

There are many reasons we should forgive. First of all, there are none among us who do not need forgiveness. In the end, we will all seek mercy, not justice. If we ourselves need to be forgiven by our fellowman, then we should also forgive when it is required of us. As we'll discuss in a minute, God's divine forgiveness of us is predicated on our forgiving our fellowman.

Secondly, if we do not forgive, our soul turns bitter, hateful, and twisted. In their book *Forgive and Love Again,* John Nieder and Thomas Thompson pointed out the destructive nature of unforgiveness. They wrote:

Unforgiveness breeds bitterness. Bitterness is a devastating sin that can be directly traced to the failure to forgive. You become caustic when you continually nurse the wound inflicted by another person. Malignant thoughts and harassing memories eventually distort how you look at life. Anger begins to rage and can easily get out of control. As your emotions begin to run wild, your mind may do the same. You entertain desperate ideas for revenge. Even casual conversations with others become your forum for slander, gossip, and innuendo against the offender. Your flesh, that horrible remnant of your old sin nature, has gained control.[1]

Forgiveness—Unique to Christianity

As Christians Jesus only gave us one option if we want God's forgiveness: we *must* forgive each other. Millions of Christians around the world repeat Sunday after Sunday: "Forgive us our debts, as we also have forgiven our debtors" (Matt. 6:12).

One time Jerry's father, who in his second career was a professor of accounting at De Paul University in Chicago, was talking with a Sikh student at a time when Sikhs and Hindus were killing each other over the Golden Temple in India. And Jerry's dad asked half jokingly, "What about turning the other cheek?" The student flung his test down on the table and angrily shouted, "Never!" This is not to pick on Sikhs. Terrorist acts by unforgiving people of other religions often make our headlines. In some cases violent acts of unforgiveness have taken place at the hands of professing Christians, e.g., in Northern Ireland.

> *Let us go to Calvary to learn how we may be forgiven. And then let us linger there to learn how we may forgive.*
>
> —Charles Spurgeon

Of all the religions in the world, none has a God that forgives except the God of the Bible, and none has the teaching of our need to forgive others. Christians, of course, have never lived up to the Christian ideal. We still don't. But that doesn't negate that the Christian ideal stands alone when it comes to forgiveness. New Testament scholar Dr. Walter Elwell wrote that forgiveness is a uniquely Christian doctrine:

> In other religions, forgiveness does not have the same force. In animism, there is no awareness of a personal relationship with God. In Hinduism, all have to pay the inexorable consequences of karma in the wheel of rein-carnations. Buddhism likewise knows nothing of a forgiving God. The idea is present in Islam, but there is no personal God and father. Even in Judaism, forgiveness as developed in the New Testament adds dimension to the teaching of the Old Testament.[2]

Aspects of Christian Forgiveness

Consider for a moment characteristics of God's forgiveness: God forgives fully and completely.

- "As far as the east is from the west, so far has he removed our transgressions from us" (Ps. 103:12).
- "You will cast all our sins / Into the depths of the sea" (Mic. 7:19b, NKJV).
- "For I will forgive their wickedness / and will remember their sins no more" (Jer. 31:34b).
- "If we confess our sins, he is faithful and just and will forgive us our sins and purify us from all unrighteousness" (1 John 1:9).

God's complete forgiveness is beautifully illustrated in the parable of the prodigal son. When the renegade son finally came to his senses, repented, and returned home, his father welcomed him with open arms and called for the fatted calf to be brought out to celebrate his son's return (Luke 15:11–32).

When the son came home (a sincere act of repentance), the father forgave completely.

Complete forgiveness is an ongoing process. It is a *must* and a way of life for every Christian, for without forgiving each other, we cannot receive God's forgiveness. Right after teaching the Lord's Prayer in the Sermon on the Mount, Jesus drove home the point of "forgive us *as we forgive others*" forcefully: "For if you forgive men when they sin against you, your heavenly Father will also forgive you. But if you do not forgive men their sins, your Father will not forgive your sins" (Matt. 6:14–15).

> *Every one says forgiveness is a lovely idea, until they have something to forgive.*
>
> —C. S. Lewis, *Mere Christianity*

How many times have our prayers been hindered or unanswered because we have not been willing to forgive?

Complete forgiveness means forgiving someone when they are totally wrong. The theology of Stephen's murderers was totally wrong. It blinded their eyes and corrupted their hearts. He knew they were wrong, but he forgave them anyway.

It's a lot easier to give lip service to forgiveness than it is to actually put it into practice. Nieder and Thompson point out that there's nothing halfhearted about real forgiveness:

> "Forgive and forget"—it sounds appealing, but the reality is missing. We can forgive. But let's be very honest: in the most literal sense of the word, we can never forget what happened. Voluntary, selective amnesia would be wonderful, but our efficient minds were not designed to forget on command. . . . Because forgiveness arouses emotions in us that are difficult to handle, we can act out our forgiveness halfheartedly and even become flippant with our words. In your frustration and inner turmoil you may be tempted to simply say, "Okay, I forgive him. Now leave me alone." If the exercise is

shallow or frivolous, it will be void of real meaning. Don't call that forgiveness. You can't forgive halfheart-edly. You can't forgive while you are emotionally dis-engaged. You can't reduce forgiveness to a simple nod of the head. Casual consent won't cut it. Forgiveness *is* a big deal. You must honestly involve your heart and your mind with what happened, and then, and only then, can you truly forgive.[3]

God Initiated Forgiveness

God takes the initiative to forgive. He does not wait for us to come to Him. In the story of the prodigal son, cited earlier, notice that the Father did not wait to see how the son was going to behave before he took him back. As God takes the first step towards us, so we are called to take the first step towards each other.

> *Someone once said, the wisest thing one can do to an enemy is to make him your friend.*
>
> —Lee Buck

Going to another person first, when he is the one who has wronged us, requires us to give up our right to be angry. There was a married couple who had been happily married for many years. When asked their secret, they confessed that when they first got married each one made up a list of ten things that they could not abide their spouse doing, and if the spouse did them, the marriage would be over. They never showed their lists to each other. As happens in mar-riages from time to time, one of them would get hopping mad at the other. When this happened, they would shout, "Lucky for you it's not on the list." Giving up our right to be angry brings us to the third characteristic of God's forgiveness.

God's forgiveness is self-sacrificing. To accomplish our for-giveness, God made the supreme sacrifice of sending His only Son.

Jesus gave up His heavenly rights, and while on earth, He gave up all of His human rights as well.

When you forgive someone, you must be willing to do them a kindness. The Bible speaks of "going the second mile" of "turning the other cheek." Doing a service sets both you and the other person free from resentment and hatred. I cannot stay mad at someone I have served or sacrificed for.

> *"When you're stabbed in the back, turn the other shoulder blade.' I had discovered that people are not my enemies— only misunderstandings and wrong thoughts are."*
>
> —Lee Buck

God wants us to be imitators of Him, so in the same way He forgives us, we should be forgiving each other. By way of review, that means:

- *We should forgive fully and completely.* This includes forgetting, forgiving an unlimited numbers of times, and forgiving even if the other person is completely wrong. We should make forgiveness for ourselves and others a part of our daily prayers. We should try to be like the father in the parable of the prodigal son and not like the unforgiving servant.

- *We should take the initiative and not wait for the other person to come to us first.* Probably the best single thing I got out of attending a Bill Gothard seminar some twenty years ago was something like this: even if your brother was 95 percent wrong and you were 5 percent wrong, go and *sincerely* ask for forgiveness for the 5 percent you are responsible for (without expecting him to ask for forgiveness for the 95 percent). Very often they will respond in kind and ask for forgiveness. But that's their responsibility. Your responsibility is to clear up the 5 percent. This is applied Christianity.

• *We should be gracious, compassionate, and self-sacrificing.*

> *Does loving your enemy mean not punishing him? No, for loving myself does not mean that I ought not to subject myself to punishment.*
>
> —C. S. Lewis, *Mere Christianity*

The Origin of the Word *Forgive*

It's very interesting to examine the origin of the word *forgive*. It comes from the Middle English word *forgifen,* which meant "to give up, to remit." This in turn came from the Anglo-Saxon *for,* which meant "away" and *gifan,* which meant "to give." When you forgive, you "give away," i.e., you give up resentment against or the desire to punish.

Real-Life Stories of People Who Learned to Forgive

There are many real-life stories of people who learned to forgive, and as examples for us to follow, we'd like to share a few.

In her book, *First We Have Coffee,* Margaret Jensen tells of how her mother forgave her

> *Forgiveness is the fragrance the violet sheds on the heel that crushed it.*
>
> —Mark Twain

father a terrible deed. Her father John was a poor pastor and very frustrated because he was situated in rural Wisconsin and preferred to be in urban New York so he could have access to good books. Her mother Mary longed to have a new dress, so she carefully saved pennies for months to purchase material from which she could sew a dress. When she finally put it together, instead of

---

Forgive your enemies,
but never forget their names.

—Attributed to John F. Kennedy

Love your enemies.

—Jesus Christ

---

pleasing him, it made him angry. In frustration (and not knowing the background of her painstaking savings and work to acquire the dress), he slashed the dress to worthless pieces. Mary then began to devise some plans to leave her husband, but soon after, during a church service wherein a visiting pastor spoke on the command for us to forgive, she decided to do so. When she returned home, she took the shredded dress and with tears put it in the old-fashioned stove as an act of forgiveness. He came into the room to find out what she was doing. When he saw the dress in flames, he remembered and apologized, and they both made up. It was this type of love and forgiveness that made their relationship last for fifty-eight mostly joyful years.[4]

In 1987 millions of viewers watched television interviews with Gordon Wilson. He and his daughter were buried in a bomb blast in North Ireland. He was holding her hand as she died. But he refused to be angry with the bombers. "I shall pray for them tonight and every night," he said. "God forgive them, for they don't know what they do."[5]

Here's a story of forgiveness told by a missionary. A white set-
tler in South Africa found a native of the Kaffir tribe near his stable
and accused him of trying to steal a horse. The native declared that
he was simply taking a shortcut home, but the white man was not
a Christian; he had no faith in Kaffirs, and he decided he would
make them afraid of him. So he tied the poor native to a tree and
cut off his right hand. Months afterward, the white man was overtaken by darkness and a storm far from his cabin. Seeking shelter
in a Kaffir hut, he was given food and a place to sleep. When he
awoke, a tall Kaffir was standing over him. As their eyes met, the
native held up his arm without a hand. The white man felt his time
had come. He knew the Kaffirs were cruel and revengeful. He
waited, expecting each moment to be his last. Slowly the right arm
dropped, and the Kaffir said: "This is my cabin and you are in my
power. You have maimed me for life, and revenge is sweet; but I
am a Christian, and I forgive you."[6]

Here's a classic story of forgiveness well worth repeating.
Corrie ten Boom, a Dutch woman, was fifty years old when World
War II broke out. She felt it was her duty to help Jews escape from
the Nazis (as did thousands of Christians in Europe). She and her
family would hide them in their home. As a result, the Nazis sent
her and her sister Betsy to Ravensbruck concentration camp,
where Betsy died. After the war, Corrie worked tirelessly helping
people to come to Christ, a part of which includes forgiveness.
Then one day, the big test came. She met a guard who had been

---

Dear God

*I know you are supposed to love thy neighbor
but if Mark keeps taking my skate he's going
to get it.*

—Kevin
From Eric Marshall and Stuart Hample, *Children's Letters to God*

at their camp. He was no longer mean and sadistic because he had found the Lord. He approached her with a beaming face and wanted to shake her hand. All the horrors of the camp, including her sister's death, passed before her eyes. Her arm seemed to be glued to her side. Silently, she prayed, "Jesus, I cannot forgive him. Give me your forgiveness." Later she wrote, "As I took his hand, the most incredible thing happened. From my shoulder, along my arm, and through my hand, a current seemed to pass from me to him, while in my heart sprang a love for this stranger that almost overwhelmed me."[7]

> *Doing an injury puts you below your enemy; revenging one makes you but even with him; forgiving it sets you above him.*
>
> —Benjamin Franklin

Conclusion

King Louis XII of France had many foes prior to his ascension to the throne. When he became king, it's reported that he made a list of his many enemies and marked each one with a large black cross. When they learned of it, his enemies fled, thinking it was his intention to avenge them. However, he "recalled" them and let it be known that "he had placed a cross beside their names to remind him of the cross that brings pardon to all: and he urged them by his own example, and especially by the example of him who prayed for his enemies, to go and do likewise."[8] The world will never hear a greater act of forgiveness than the words of Christ on the cross: "Father, forgive them for they know not what they do." And so, if we want to avoid the deadly sin of anger, we must learn to forgive.

chapter 11

Lust

Our lusts are cords that bind us.

—Charles Spurgeon

He was an honorable man, a man of wisdom and maturity. His career path had catapulted him from humble origins working out in the fields watching dumb animals all the way to the top post in his country. A skilled musician and a well-liked man, he was a Renaissance man centuries before the Renaissance. He also had a strong relationship with his God. Nonetheless, one night, in a moment of weakness, he ended up showing the world that he too had feet of clay. I'm referring, of course, to King David and what happened when lust got the better of him.

One spring, when kings were supposed to go off to war, he stayed home in Jerusalem. That's when he saw her. One night, unable to sleep, he had gone for a walk on the flat roof of the palace. She was on her own roof, taking a bath. When he looked at her, he saw she was very beautiful, and he couldn't get her out of his mind. So began the torrid affair of David and Bathsheba, which was to have devastating consequences (2 Sam. 11).

This chapter will look at lust and analyze its destructive impact. Since what happened with David provides an excellent example of what to avoid in this realm, we will return at various times to his story in this chapter.

> *If you are thinking to yourself, 'An affair could never happen to me,' you are in trouble. To believe that we are immune leaves us wide open and unprotected.*
>
> —Ellen Williams

Lust Wages War with the Soul

The most important thing I'd like to say at the outset is that lust battles with our very souls. We are aliens and strangers in this world. If you're a Christian—that is, if you've been born anew, born again, born "from above"—then ultimately heaven is your real home. This world is something we're just passing through. That sounds so much like a cliché, but it's a truth that we should remind ourselves of from time to time.

The Bible warns us that since we are aliens and strangers here we should avoid lusts because they wage war with the soul. I think that's a good description. First Peter 2:11 states: "Dear friends, I urge you, as foreigners and strangers in the world, to abstain from sinful desires, which war against your soul."

How many times do people fall away from Christ because their lusts drag them down? I think it's rather common. I can think of people who claim they fell away from Christ because there was some alleged deficiency with Christianity. But the reality is that it was *lust* that got the better of them. For example, one famous anti-Christian humanist of today claims he left the church because God didn't answer his prayers, yet at the same time he "had a girl in every port," to quote *Time* magazine. Psychologists describe a condition known as "cognitive dissonance," which is a fancy way of describing the idea that you can't hold two mutually exclusive beliefs at the same time for too long. Eventually, one will win out over the other. Either you have to admit that your sexual behavior is wrong and stop it (or at least make the commitment to stop it) or you have to say it's OK and stop pretending to be a Christian. In the realm of lust, if a professing Christian gives himself over to his sensual desires without restraint and becomes a slave to them, he feels terribly guilty and very uncomfortable with being identified as a Christian. The one battles the other. One may win over the other for a time and then vice versa. It's critical that we recognize the damaging effects that lust can have on our faith.

Even the one-time godly man, King Solomon, had a serious problem with lust (as we'll briefly explore later):

"I find more bitter than death
the woman who is a snare,
whose heart is a trap
and whose hands are chains.
The man who pleases God will escape her,
but the sinner she will ensnare" (Eccles. 7:26).

Lust was a key part of his downfall.

I can think of a handful of Christians I've known *personally* that fell away primarily because lust got the best of them. Think of some well-known Christian leaders who lost powerful ministries that they toiled to build up for years, all because of a moment of weakness. While God *forgives* those who repent, there are still the *consequences* we pay for our sin. The tragedy is, despite the well-publicized falls of televangelists Jim Bakker and Jimmy Swaggart, there are still all sorts of lesser known Christian leaders whose ministries topple because they lose the battle with lust. This area, perhaps more than any other, has the ability to destroy lives, families, churches; and, as we'll see in David's case, even a nation can be hurt by one man's sexual sins. Lust does indeed wage war with the soul.

The Anatomy of Lust

Lust begins in the mind. When a man views sexually explicit materials, hormones are released that burn these images into his brain. Like harmful LSD flashbacks, they can reoccur, drawing him deeper and deeper into a world of fantasy. In the book *An Affair of the Mind,* author Laurie Hall described the effect pornography had on her husband. He had kept his addiction hidden from her during the eighteen years of their marriage, but she knew something was wrong. He spent too much time away from home, did not pay their bills, at times became catatonic, and eventually lost his job. She wrote:

> One day, when I was agonizing in prayer, asking the Lord to show me what was going on, He gave me a picture of Jack's brain. It was completely smooth except for one terribly deep trench that ran down one side. I knew instinctively that the trench was the fantasy track in his mind. The trench was so deep that there didn't

Sex, sex, sex. Our culture is near the point of total saturation. The cesspool is running over. Books, magazines, billboards, movies shout it ceaselessly. TV, the most powerful and immediate medium, trumpets it in living color. Sex gets the ratings. It is the recurring theme in daytime soaps and talk shows, the inevitable subject in the nighttime interviews.

—J. Allan Peterson

seem to be any way out of it. The rest of his brain, I could see, was virtually unused. Jack had blown his mind on fantasy.[1]

This information was later confirmed in a counseling session with Dr. Ron Miller:

After examining Jack, Dr. Miller looked at him and said, "You've destroyed your mind by fantasizing. You've dug a deep channel going in one direction. The rest of your mind has atrophied."[2]

This man nearly lost his family because of his pornography. He certainly lost a great deal of respect and success:

Once a regional manager for a large company, over-seeing millions of dollars worth of equipment and managing half a dozen men, Jack had an expense account, a cellular phone, a company vehicle, and a comfortable middle-class salary. Today, he is doing production work, packing 12-ounce bags of chocolates at $7.25 an hour. He stands at an assembly line seven-and-a-half hours a day, catching bags that come off the machine at a rate of 71 a minute. Then he puts them into boxes— 24 to a box. Sometimes, he scrapes chocolate off the factory floor.[3]

Uncontrolled lust brought him from the heights down to the pits.

Did You Know?

One out of five Americans (more than 56 million of us) has a viral sexually transmitted disease, such as gonorrhea, syphilis, chlamydia, and herpes.

—Miami Herald

Lust Is a Woman's Problem Too

Lust is not only a man's problem; women have it too, but it takes another form. The chemical reaction does not take place in her brain by what she *sees* but by what she *feels* emotionally. She wants to be wanted. A man in lust sends out brain waves that say, "I want." A woman interprets this incorrectly as meaning, "I want you." The signals are like strong radio waves and can travel for miles. They act like a magnet drawing her to him and can turn her brain into virtual mush. She can become as pliable as a radio-controlled model airplane. She reasons, *If he wants me that much, it must be love.* Sometimes lust turns into love, but most of the time it does not.

Lustful men who have discovered they have this power to magnetize women keep their transmitter continually broadcasting. They may not be good-looking, but they attract an amazing number of women who are absolutely obsessed with them.

> *Probably the basic lie of Satan underlying all of his deceptions is that the laws of God will restrict and narrow and diminish one's life. How many people have sadly learned that just the opposite is the truth, when their bodies have been vitiated by venereal disease, or their minds have been scrambled by various guilt-induced psychoses or neuroses, and found, only too late, that had they followed God's path their life would have been enriched and ennobled?*
>
> —D. James Kennedy

Lust is bad because God says so. It has devastating effects on our lives, our families, our souls. Lust is obsessive. A man becomes obsessed with how a woman looks, and a woman with how a man makes her feel. Each knows how to intensify the obsession of the other, and they think they are madly "in love." How many lives have been ruined because a man and a woman thought they were in love, when they were only disastrously "in lust"? Tragically, people often lack discernment when it comes to the line between love and infatuation. Love and infatuation are entirely different species.

What Does the Bible Say About Lust?

For starters, the tenth commandment (Exod. 20:17) prohibits lust: "You shall not covet your neighbor's wife." Lust can easily lead to breaking the seventh commandment (Exod. 20:14): "You shall not commit adultery."

Proverbs 2:16–19 warns of the consequences of lusting after the immoral woman:

"For her house leads down to death,
  and her paths to the spirits of the dead" (v. 18).

Proverbs 5 describes the guile of the immoral woman and urges men to avoid her like the plague:

For the lips of an adulteress drip honey,
  and her speech is smoother than oil;
but in the end she is bitter as gall,
  sharp as a double-edged sword.
Her feet go down to death;
  her steps lead straight to the grave.
She gives no thought to the way of life;
  her paths are crooked, but she knows it not.
Now then, my sons, listen to me;
  do not turn aside from what I say.
Keep to a path far from her,
  do not go near the door of her house,

lest you give your best strength to others and
>your years to one who is cruel,
lest strangers feast on your wealth
>and your toil enrich another man's house.
At the end of your life you will groan,
>when your flesh and body are spent.
You will say, "How I hated discipline!
>How my heart spurned correction!
I would not obey my teachers
>or listen to my instructors.
I have come to the brink of utter ruin
>in the midst of the whole assembly" (Prov. 5:3–14).

Is there anything new under the sun? These practical words are defied virtually every day in living color just on the soap operas. In such dramas, perhaps there will be happy resolutions to people living in sin; in real life, the consequences are usually devastating.

Lustful fantasies unchecked will invariably lead to some sort of outlet, including an adulterous affair. I keep saying "unchecked" or "uncontrolled" because to some degree we all struggle with the temptation to lust. The key is whether it reigns in us or not.

Origins of the Word *Pornography*

The word *pornography* has an interesting relationship with adultery. *Porno* means "harlot" or "prostitute." *Graph* means "picture." So pornography consists of pictures of prostitutes. Thus, Solomon's warning of not physically going to the adulteress applies to the same idea of not looking at pornography, for in so doing, you could actually be taking the first step toward the adulteress described in this passage.

Proverbs 6 also warns against adultery, as does Proverbs 7. Proverbs 6:27–29 reminds us that lust has dire consequences from which we will not escape:

"Can a man scoop fire into his lap
>without his clothes being burned?

Can a man walk on hot coals/without his feet being
scorched?
So is he who sleeps with another man's wife;
no one who touches her will go unpunished."

Proverbs 7:27 says of the adulteress:

"Her house is a highway to the grave,
leading down to the chambers of death."

All the above notwithstanding, the key scriptural teaching on
lust is found in the Sermon on the Mount (Matt. 5:27–28): "You
have heard that it was said, 'Do not commit adultery.' But I tell you
that anyone who looks at a woman lustfully has already committed adultery with her in his heart." Some people mistakenly talk
about Jimmy Carter's comments about "lust in the heart" as if he
had made up the whole concept; but, of course, he was merely cit-
ing what Jesus talked about in the Sermon on the Mount.

Jesus knew that sexual sin starts in the mind. He meant we
should not indulge ourselves in thoughts that, if acted out, would
break moral laws. He meant that we should discipline our
thoughts. This is stated even more strongly in Colossians 3:5: "Put
to death, therefore, whatever belongs to your earthly nature: sexual immorality, impurity, lust, evil desires and greed, which is
idolatry."

According to Old Testament law, if a man and woman were
caught in the act of adultery, both were to be stoned to death.
There was a stiff penalty for
physical adultery in part
because it snared another person into sin. Jesus was not saying that physical adultery and
mental adultery are the same.
His point was that both are sexual sins, and we are responsible
for both. And the inward reality
(lust in the heart) can lead to
the outward reality (adultery).

> *I broke your laws*
> *[regarding sex], but I*
> *did not escape your*
> *scourges. For what*
> *mortal man can do*
> *that?*
>
> —St. Augustine

Jesus knew the obsessive nature of lust and that sooner or later we will all be tempted by it. Therefore, He gave this stern warning to guard against it.

An Intriguing Analogy from C. S. Lewis

My favorite Christian writer C. S. Lewis, the Oxford and later Cambridge professor, once made an interesting point about sex and our culture's fascination with it. Keep in mind, this was written in England in a book with a 1960 copyright. How far we have degenerated from that time to the present in our modern "liberated" views on sex. Said Mr. Lewis,

> You can get a large audience together for a strip-tease act—that is, to watch a girl undress on the stage. Now suppose you came to a country where you could fill a theatre by simply bringing a covered plate on to the stage and then slowly lifting the cover so as to let everyone see, just before the lights went out, that it contained a mutton chop or a bit of bacon, would you not think that in that country something had gone wrong with the appetite for food?[4]

Clearly, there is something sick about the way our normal appetite for sex has been so twisted and distorted in our time. I remember being in a large American city one Friday evening. We drove past some nudie bars that catered to heterosexuals and another one that catered to homosexuals.[5] Both places were packed, and their businesses were flourishing,

> *Better shun the bait than struggle in the snare.*
>
> —John Dryden

and it struck me that this means there must be a lot of unhappy people that don't have a good sex life at home (if they're married at all).

A World Saturated with Lust

We live in a world where lust is rampant. Americans spend approximately $12 to $13 billion per year on pornography.[6] This includes pornographic videos, magazines, and phone sex. Laurie Hall pointed out: "That's more money than if you combined the annual revenues of the Coca-Cola and the McDonnell Douglas corporations."[7]

Young people are being bombarded with temptation in this area, perhaps like never before. To my knowledge, the $12 to $13 billion figure would not include other more "soft" forms of pornography as found in examples such as some R-rated films or bikini issues of sports' magazines and the like.

Unfortunately, Christian teens are reportedly watching just about as many of the R-rated films as non-Christian teens, according to Dr. Ted Baehr, president of The Christian Film and Television Commission.[8] Furthermore, a recent Barna poll showed that "Christian young adults are more likely than others to have watched *MTV* in the past week."[9] For example, Barna has found that 42 percent of Christian "baby busters" (the generation that followed the "baby boomers") watch *MTV* versus only 33 percent of non-Christian baby busters. That's not good, especially in light of the many lustful images portrayed in this kind of programming.

Ours is a culture with a serious lust problem. Sex is used to market all sorts of products. While we have had an open and permissive view toward sex, people are developing all sorts of sexual hang-ups. With computers and the Internet, people are able to communicate instantaneously with people on the other side of the world. And yet, some of the most often-visited websites are those that contain pornography; the Internet is even used sometimes by sexual predators seeking their prey. There's a noisy, powerful homosexual lobby, urging people to live their lives by their glands and lusts, rather than by Judeo-Christian standards of right and wrong. The problem of abortion that plagues this nation is the natural outworking of the Playboy philosophy. It's the way many people try to cover up their sin. In short, we have a real problem with lust.

But, is there anything new under the sun? Not really. The problem of lust has plagued mankind from the beginning.

David and Bathsheba

Suppose we could take away all the external stimuli currently available in our culture. David and Bathsheba lived in an age when there were no X-rated movies, no porn shops, no erotic magazines, no escort services, yet they fell. Lust is an age-old problem.

If David had not stayed away from where he was supposed to be (the battlefield), his lust would not have had the opportunity to grow. All we know about Bathsheba is that she was alone and that she was beautiful. Her husband Uriah was away at war, defending his country against the Ammonites. When David saw her bathing, he noted her beauty and called for her. She did not have much choice in the matter. The king could get what the king wanted. However, I will add that David was generally sensitive to the things of God so that had she put up an argument appealing to David's sense of right and wrong, I speculate he would have listened and could have stopped the whole sordid affair before it even began.

With Bathsheba, David's lust now grew into full-blown adultery. This was to have devastating consequences on his children, especially Amnon, Absalom, Tamar, and Solomon.

When Bathsheba informed David that she was pregnant with his child, David eventually decided to have Uriah killed in battle to cover up his sin. (2 Sam. 11:14–17). Thus, David's lust led first to adultery and then it led to murder. (And some look at lust as if it's a new problem.)

Thankfully, David eventually repented—after about a year. He faced his adultery because Nathan the prophet called it to his attention. God was displeased with David. He not only sent the prophet, but David and Bathsheba's baby also died. Although he was forgiven, David had to live with the devastating consequences of his

Family counselor J. Allan Peterson, who warned against adultery in his marvelous book, The Myth of the Greener Grass, *pointed out eight noteworthy lessons from David's adultery:*

1. No one, however chosen, blessed, and used of God, is immune to an extramarital affair.

2. Anyone, regardless of how many victories he has won, can fall disastrously.

3. The act of infidelity is the result of uncontrolled desires, thoughts, and fantasies.

4. Your body is your servant or it becomes your master.

5. A Christian who falls will excuse, rationalize, and conceal, the same as anyone else.

6. Sin can be enjoyable, but it can never be successfully covered.

7. One night of passion can spark years of family pain.

8. Failure is neither fatal nor final.

—J. Allan Peterson, *The Myth of the Greener Grass*

sin. To make matters worse, some of his children got caught up in imitation of his evil deeds.

One son, Amnon, raped one of David's beautiful daughters, Tamar, who had a different mother than Amnon, her half brother. In revenge, Tamar's brother, Absalom, eventually murdered his half brother Amnon for raping his sister.

Amnon's rape was motivated by what we could call a textbook case of lust. Before he finally raped her, Amnon lusted for her for a long, long time. He was absolutely obsessed by her beauty. Amnon couldn't get Tamar out of his mind. She dominated his thoughts. He must have turned over and over in his mind all the sexual fantasies of what he wanted to do with her a thousand times

> *Samson, for all his strong body, had a weak head, or he would not have laid it in a harlot's lap.*
>
> —Benjamin Franklin

before he actually raped her. His "love" for her was so strong that he became physically ill.

Then, after he raped her, there was a big change in his mentality. The Bible says that he now hated her more than he had loved her. This is a powerful illustration of lust in action. Amnon had not been "in love" with Tamar. He had been "in lust" with her.

Absalom, Amnon's half brother and executioner, also manifested lustful behavior. When he seized David's kingdom at one point in an armed rebellion, one of the steps he took to defy his father was to sleep with his father's concubines (2 Sam. 16:22). Unfortunately, David's children were following their father's example—the *wrong* example.

King Solomon, David's successor, was also to manifest a serious problem with lust. Surely, Solomon's lust went far beyond David's obsession for another man's wife or Amnon's obsession for his sister. Solomon amassed seven hundred wives and three hundred concubines (1 Kings 11:3). With such a harem, he could have sex every night with a different woman for three years straight. It's inconceivable that he could have achieved intimacy under such an arrangement.

Kings were forbidden to marry foreign women (Deut. 7:3–4). Attached to the command was the warning that doing so would turn their hearts from the Lord, and the Lord would destroy them suddenly. Solomon disobeyed this command. He married foreign wives to seal trade agreements, to prevent wars, and in general, to expand his kingdom.

Solomon had enthusiastically followed God in his youth. Solomon built a beautiful temple and worshiped there regularly. He wrote portions of Scripture, most notably, the bulk of Proverbs.

But as he married more foreign wives, he began to drift away from God. To keep peace in the family, he built each wife an altar for her own god. This made God angry, and because of his sin, the kingdom would be split in two—a prophecy (1 Kings 11:31) that was fulfilled under the reign of Solomon's son and successor, Rehoboam. Rehoboam is described as an evil king. During his reign, worship of the true God disappeared from the land for the most part. Instead, the people practiced all the abominations of the nations that the Lord had driven out, including the use of male and female temple prostitutes (1 Kings 14:24).

Thus we see that in only three generations—David, Solomon, and Rehoboam—a kingdom was destroyed in many ways by lust. Largely from a simple glance down at a bathing beauty. What we do in secret does affect others, particularly our children. David not only passed his values on to the next generation; he passed on his sins as well.[10]

Empirical Data Correlates with God's Word

The most comprehensive study on sex in America to date was the one conducted in 1992 and released in 1993 by the National Opinion Research Center, which is affiliated with the University of Chicago. It exploded many myths about sex. They found that the group presented on the media—young, unmarried singles—as having the "hottest sex" were often the group least likely to have regular sex. In contrast, "boring" married couples who were faithful to each other were the ones having sex most often and with greater satisfaction. The researchers wrote:

> Once again contradicting the common view of marriage as dull and routine, the people who reported being the most physically pleased and emotionally satisfied were the married couples. . . . The lowest rates of satisfaction were among men and women who were neither married nor living with someone—the very group thought to be having the hottest sex.[11]

The study found over and over that marriage—not fornication, not adultery—brought the greatest sexual fulfillment of all.[12] Thankfully, they also found that adultery in practice was not the norm in America.[13]

Conclusion

A battle often rages—a battle in our minds—a battle between lust and purity. Randy Alcorn wrote, "The enemy is lust, the stakes are high, the reward is the peace and pleasure of purity."[14]

Back in the 1980s, dozens of witnesses were called to testify before the Attorney General's Commission on Pornography. This included many victims of the so-called "victimless crime." With the words of one of those victims, we close out the chapter, pointing out once more that lust wages war with the soul: "Pornography and spirituality do not coexist. If a person is spiritually aware, he has respect for himself and others. Pornography sells and feeds off of disrespect for self and others."[15]

Purity

*The body is the soul's image;
therefore keep it pure.*

—Pope Xystus I

A Christian writer was perplexed by the number of occasions he was aware of where pastors committed adultery. This bothered him, so he decided to study it and write up his findings. The essence of what he learned was that these men were acting out what they had practiced over and over in their mind's eye. They had committed adultery in their hearts repeatedly. Then when the opportunity finally made itself available in a real-life situation, they simply acted out what they had envisioned so often before. They hadn't applied the biblical truth that purity begins in the mind, that it begins in the heart.

The Bible wisely says, "Guard your heart" (Prov. 4:23). It all starts in the heart. Above all, we must avoid dwelling in our minds on temptations. Some people play (like VCR tapes) their sinful thoughts over and over. They savor them. Then when the moment for temptation comes—Bam! They give in. And then they wonder why they sinned. Guard your heart, for from it comes the issues of life. Thus it's important not to flood our minds with those things that will entice our natural lusts. We are the ones who choose which nature we'll feed—the old one or the new one. We're the ones who select the food for the mind and prepare the meal. We may be tempted by lust, but that doesn't mean we have to give in. The outcome of the battle is up to us, and it all begins in the mind.

> *Never flirt—even in jest. Flirtation is intrinsically flattering. You may think you are being cute, but it often arouses unrequited desires in another.*
>
> —R. Kent Hughes, *Disciplines of a Godly Man*

God has promised He will always provide a way of escape (1 Cor. 10:13). The biggest problem is that too often we choose *not* to take that way out. I have struggled with this problem of lust quite a bit. I remember the old hymn "And Can It Be?" where it says: "my chains fell off, my heart was free, I rose, went forth and followed Thee." And then I would think, *That's right, but I have chosen to go back to those chains!* I know what's right, but I'm choosing what's wrong! Lord, help me. This is reminiscent of the struggle Paul describes in Romans 7 where he told how he knew what was right, but he did what's wrong:

> We know that the law is spiritual; but I am unspiritual, sold as a slave to sin. I do not understand what I do. For what I want to do I do not do, but what I hate I do. . . . Now if I do what I do not want to do, it is no longer I who do it, but it is sin living in me that does it. . . . What a wretched man I am! Who will rescue me from this body of death? Thanks be to God—through Jesus Christ our Lord! (Rom. 7:14–15, 20, 24–25).[1]

Obviously, Paul found freedom out of this tragic situation he described. Unfortunately, there are many who don't. As I said, it seems that the wayside is littered with Christians who have fallen in this (and perhaps other areas) and have not been able to get up. But if one truly belongs to Christ, he will get up again; even if he falls repeatedly, he will get up again.

The Bible is very practical on the matter of purity (and on all things it addresses):

> Drink water from your own cistern,
>> running water from your own well.
> Should your springs overflow in the streets,
>> your streams of water in the public squares?
> Let them be yours alone,
>> never to be shared with strangers.
> May your fountain be blessed,
>> and may you rejoice in the wife of your youth.
> A loving doe, a graceful deer—
>> may her breasts satisfy you always,
>> may you ever be captivated by her love.
> Why be captivated, my son, by an adulteress?
>> Why embrace the bosom of another man's wife?
> For a man's ways are in full view of the LORD,
>> and he examines all his paths.
> The evil deeds of a wicked man ensnare him;
>> the cords of his sin hold him fast.
> He will die for lack of discipline,
>> led astray by his own great folly (Prov. 5:15–23).

How Pervasive Is Adultery?

How uncommon is purity in our time? Here's perhaps a jaded view (and certainly not a scientific survey) but it reflects an ugly reality. When J. Allan Peterson was working on his book on adultery, appropriately entitled *The Myth of the Greener Grass*, he said:

"One working girl told me, 'I work in an office with twenty-three other wives. I am the only one still faithful to my husband. They think I'm odd—ask me what my problem is.'"[2]

Pastor R. Kent Hughes wrote,

> The sticky steam of sensuality penetrates everything in our world! . . . And the Church has not escaped, for many in today's Church have wilted under the heat. Recently *Leadership Magazine* commissioned a poll of a thousand pastors. The pastors indicated that 12 percent of them had committed adultery while in the ministry—one out of eight pastors!—and 23 percent had done something they considered sexually inappropriate. *Christianity Today* surveyed a thousand of its subscribers who were *not* pastors and found the figure to be nearly double, with 23 percent saying they had had extramarital intercourse and 45 percent indicating they had done something they themselves deemed sexually inappropriate. One in four Christian men are unfaithful, and nearly one half have behaved unbecomingly! Shocking statistics! Especially when we remember that *Christianity Today* readers tend to be college-educated church leaders, elders, deacons, Sunday school superintendents, and teachers. If this is so for the Church's leadership, how much more for the average member of the congregation. Only God knows!
>
> This leads us to an inescapable conclusion: The contemporary evangelical Church, broadly considered, is "Corinthian" to the core.[3]

> *The most effective oral contraceptive is the word no.*
>
> —Variation of a Woody Allen line

Thus, there's a great need for purity in our time.

> *Do not bare your heart to another woman, or pour forth your troubles to her. Intimacy is a great need in most people's lives—and talking about personal matters, especially one's problems, can fill another's need for intimacy, awakening a desire for more. Many affairs begin in just this way.*
>
> —R. Kent Hughes, *Disciplines of a Godly Man*

Purity Demands Discernment in What We Allow Ourselves to See

How is it that purity is so difficult to maintain? Many Christians, including myself (Jerry) have managed to ignore one of the main avenues through which lust can easily get a foothold in our lives. We have been very lax at not recognizing this foothold. I'm referring to our choices of entertainment.

It would be ridiculous to complain about giving in to temptation if you've allowed all sorts of garbage in your home. As much as we can, we must rid ourselves of all triggers to temptation, e.g., pornography, booze, cigarettes, drugs, or whatever the trigger is to your pet sin. I know of one man who gave up cable TV because there was too much of a sexual nature on television. This was a wise thing for him to do. I know of another man that doesn't go to the beach anymore because of the bathing suits (or lack thereof). He knows it will possibly cause him to fall. He knows his own limits, thus, he chooses to avoid temptation.

Many professing Christians actually watch for entertainment value some of the most offensive programs on the air. It's almost as if they temporarily put the lordship of Christ on hold for the duration of a particular program or movie. Yet David said so long ago, "I will set before my eyes no vile thing" (Ps. 101:3). In light of what we've discussed about David, I guess this is one of those pieces of advice where it's "do as I *say,* not as I *do*". But it's great advice: I will set before my eyes no vile thing. That should be our attitude when it comes to what we view. So often, all it takes is a little trigger here or there from some sort of source, and we suddenly become tempted to look at pornography or to satisfy our lust in some other way. Consider that 88 percent of sexual activity in prime-time television is between people who are not married, according to media watchdog Don Wildmon. Thus, television makes "lust more attractive than love."[4]

> *Two natures beat within*
> *my breast.*
> *The one is foul, the*
> *other is blest.*
> *The one I love,*
> *the other I hate.*
> *The one I* feed *will dominate.*
>
> —Anonymous

I'm amazed at the blind spot so many Christians have in the area of TV and movie viewing. It's almost as if their view of personal holiness doesn't take entertainment choices into consideration. They may be godly by this and that criterion, but when it comes to what movies or TV programs they see, seemingly anything goes.

Remember Job's commitment in this area? "I made a covenant with my eyes not to look lustfully at a girl" (Job 31:1). Pastor Hughes made the point that "Job's covenant forbids a second look."[5] If you just happen to see a beautiful woman, it's one thing to take in her beauty at a glance. It's another to indulge in a second (and third and fourth) glance. It's easy to get sloppy in this area, even for professing Christians.

The Role of Accountability in Maintaining Purity

None of the above is in any way said in self-righteousness. I know firsthand the enormous, attractive nature of pornography. I personally have struggled with lust. Before I became a Christian, I looked at a great deal of pornography . . . nothing out of the ordinary, like some of the really sick stuff out there. But I can honestly say I wished I had never looked at any of it. Never. When I was in high school, I secretly bought quite a few pornographic magazines. I had them stashed under my bed or later, stashed in a secret spot in the attic where they would be difficult to reach (but still accessible). When I first became born again as a freshman in college, I felt totally free in this area. But I became bitterly disappointed a few months later when I fell into this sin again. I thought, *What is wrong with me?* I struggled with this off and on, and thankfully, by God's grace, I was able to experience a great deal of victory, even in the face of situations of temptation. For example, my roommate in college who was an atheist had quite a collection of porn magazines, which were a snare to me at first. But after one time where

> *Men, it is impossible for you to maintain a pure mind if you are a television-watching 'couch potato.' In one week you will watch more murders, adulteries, and perversions than our grandfathers read about in their entire lives.*
>
> —R. Kent Hughes,
> *Disciplines of a Godly Man*

I nearly got caught peeking at his stash, I was totally embarrassed—since here I was the "Christian" doing something I knew was wrong and was a terrible witness. The shame and humiliation of nearly getting caught, combined with other factors, was able to keep me free from pornography for a long time. Those other factors included reminding myself, before I was tempted to fall, of the horrible waves of guilt that would wash over me if I gave in. I felt as if a porno magazine were like a piece of cheese that Satan would put on a mousetrap. Looking at it would cause the trap to snap on me. When tempted, it's helpful to look beyond the temptation to see the evil face of the tempter![6]

When I later married, I realized that pornography had bad consequences for my marriage. It brought nothing positive to the bedroom, only negative thoughts, since the average wife doesn't usually live up to the images portrayed in such magazines. (Many times, those women themselves don't live up to those images. Minor imperfections on their bodies are airbrushed away. I've even heard about the beautiful legs of one woman being photographically dubbed in to replace the less-than-perfect legs of a model that looks good from the waist up.) The women in these magazines smile at you. But are they really that friendly? It's all an illusion.

> *I have seen men who once, then repeatedly, 'sneak a look' at pornography and are drawn toward adultery. Often they lose their sexual attraction to the one woman God has given them to enjoy sex with. I have also seen the low self-esteem of real women who have lost their husbands to the fantasy nymphs of* Playboy *and Hollywood.*
>
> —Randy C. Alcorn

In my struggle with pornography, through the years—by God's grace—I have basically managed to keep lust in check. I remember in particular one turning point, a moment of great temptation, where God indeed provided a very clear way out.

One time, more than ten years ago, I was in a New York City hotel on assignment for a television ministry. Unlike our normal custom, I was alone and separated from our crew for a few days. During that time, with pornography all around me, I came under heavy temptation. One night in particular, I felt tempted to go and purchase a pornographic magazine. No one would know, except God of course. But I got down on my knees, and I prayed for His help to stay pure. Amazingly, the more I prayed, the more powerless I seemed over this thing! I began to feel resigned to temptation. I must confess that I literally stood up with the intention in my heart of deliberately sinning. *But then came the way of escape.*

The phone rang. It turned out to be a freelance producer who happened to be in town. He was there to scout out locations for our next project. I knew nothing about his being in New York City. He asked me if I could join him that night in scouting out certain sites in Manhattan. I was glad to. When we got together, I asked him if he would do me a favor. Would he ask me the next morning if I looked at anything I shouldn't have? I asked him to ask me if I even turned on the TV. Keep in mind this was in 1988 when independent TV stations across Middle America were showing uncut, R-rated movies. If they were showing such movies on prime time in Kansas, what were they showing after dark in New York City hotels? So I decided not to even turn on the television there, lest I open myself up to temptation. So my colleague promised to hold me accountable. Just knowing that he was going to ask me the next morning about all these things kept me pure. I learned that night a very important lesson in this area: godly accountability. If you struggle with lust, find a trusted brother to whom you can report at least once a week on how well you did that week. This can help free us from a lifetime of bad habits.

Purity Comes About Through the Renewing of Our Minds

Ultimately, there is no greater way to bring about purity in our lives than by the renewing of our minds. And there's no greater way to achieve that than through the Word of God—meditating upon it, memorizing passages, mulling these things over in our minds. We will, it seems, mull over something. It makes much more sense to mull over the Bible. How can a young man keep his way pure? By living according to God's Word (See Ps. 119:9).

If lust is one of your root sins, then here's a passage worth memorizing and turning over and over in your mind:

> It is God's will that you should be sanctified: that you should avoid sexual immorality; that each of you should learn to control his own body in a way that is holy and honorable, not in passionate lust like the heathen, who do not know God; and that in this matter no one should wrong his brother or take advantage of him. The Lord will punish men for all such sins (1 Thess. 4:3–6).

You often hear Christians say something to the effect, "Oh, if only I knew the will of God for my life!" I want to say to them that this passage at least partially answers their professed longing: it is God's will for you to be holy.

Can We Retain Purity Once We've Lost It?

Can someone who has committed sexual sin ever be pure again? Many who have fallen into sexual sin are so addicted they do not want to be pure. They just want to drag others down into the same slimy pit, and thus they work hard to snag as many victims as possible.

But what about those who have truly repented—the ones who have said, "I don't want to be like that anymore." Is there any hope

> *A man who constantly gave in to the temptation of pornography was told to memorize five Bible verses relating to that temptation. When Satan attacked that weakness again, he was to quote each of those verses three times. When the mailman delivered a pornographic magazine to his apartment by mistake, the man was tempted. But after quoting those five verses for three times each, he had the strength to throw the magazine away without even opening it! He planned a defense, replaced his sinful thoughts with Scripture, and saw victory for the first time!*
>
> —*Truths that Transform,* Coral Ridge Ministries

for them? Suppose a young teenage girl decides it was wrong to sleep with her boyfriend and vows abstinence until marriage. Suppose a salesman decides to stop sleeping with prostitutes while he is on the road. Suppose a drag queen decides to hang up the dresses and play it straight for the rest of his life. Purity is possible, but let us make sure we understand what it is.

1. *Purity is not the same thing as innocence.* If we have fallen, we cannot go back to being innocent. But we can move forward toward maintaining purity now and in the future.

- Innocence is acting the right way before you have fallen for the wrong way.
- Purity is acting the right way after you have fallen for the wrong way.

Sexual sin can leave us feeling as unclean as lepers. Understanding the difference between innocence and purity can give us courage to live God's way, no matter what we have done in the past. Billy Graham once said, "You can't unscramble scrambled eggs." That is to say, you can't undo the sin in your life prior to the time you came to Christ. Or even if we've blown it as a Christian, we can't undo our unholiness of the past. But we can work toward being holy in the present and future. A lie of the devil is that since we've blown it, that's it—it's time for God to put us on the "never to be used again" shelf.[7] That's very untrue. Despite many ways we may have blown it, it's

> *Purity is not the same thing as innocence. Just because we may have lost our innocence—which we can never regain once lost—doesn't mean we can't maintain our purity.*

His desire we come back to Him and receive forgiveness and cleansing. We need to use "the Christian's bar of soap": "If we confess our sins, He is faithful and righteous to forgive us our sins and to cleanse us from all unrighteousness" (1 John 1:9, NASB).

2. *God does not require us to return to innocence.* When Adam and Eve disobeyed God by tasting the forbidden fruit, God did not take away the knowledge they had gained. He did not give them a lobotomy so they would forget they were naked. Rather, He covered their sin by killing an animal from which he made animal skins as clothing for them. He killed the animal because the only way sin can be covered is by the shedding of blood. Our sexual sins are covered by the blood of Jesus because He died on the cross and paid the penalty for them.

3. *Loss of innocence brings consequences.* Don't think that Adam and Eve got off scot-free. They had to pay the consequences for what they had done. These included not being allowed to live in the garden of paradise anymore, working extra hard to earn a

living, experiencing pain in childbirth, and physical death. They did not suffer the ultimate punishment, that of being cut off from God completely and forever; but ever after, they would have to struggle more to live the right way.

4. *God requires us to maintain purity.* After we have fallen, maintaining purity requires great discipline, but that is what God wants. Jesus said to the woman caught in adultery, "Neither do I condemn you; go and sin no more" (John 8:11, NKJV). God forgives, but He expects us to toe the line.

5. *Purity is a lifelong process.* Many homosexuals believe they can never change and don't even try. (Of course, they are misinformed because homosexuality is a learned behavior and can be unlearned.) Many who have wanted to change have stopped trying. They complain, "I tried God. I tried Christianity. It didn't work." What should we say to them? An appropriate response would be, "What did you expect God to do for you?" The same applies to those struggling with heterosexual sin. Instant deliverance sometimes occurs, but it is rare. Normally, the process takes time. Over a period of several years, the frequency and intensity of their desires will diminish if they seek God first. We live in a

> *How can a young man keep his way pure?*
> *By living according to your word.*
>
> —Psalm 119:9

microwave culture, where pastors do not preach often about the realities of *struggling* with sin. Some people, I suppose, expect baptism to be a magic water that sanctifies us instantly from head to toe. However, sanctification is a lifetime process. Purity requires prayer and patient persistence.

6. *Accountability helps maintain purity.* There are many ways to maintain purity. As I pointed out earlier from firsthand experience, one of the best is accountability: reporting to someone we

trust on a regular basis. Men in our culture are raised to be independent and accountable to no one. This is wrong-headed. It leads to blind spots, inflated egos, and the cultivation of secret and/or full-blown addictions that can destroy our souls. In the last few years, men have come to realize the importance of being held accountable. Thank God for Promise Keepers. They have started forming accountability groups that meet on a weekly basis in which they hold one

> *I have hidden your word in my heart that I might not sin against you.*
>
> —Psalm 119:11

another accountable morally, spiritually, and financially. They confess their shortcomings and pray for one another. If you struggle with this, find someone you can trust and to whom you will be honest. It could be as simple as a five-minute phone call once a week. Just knowing you'll have to answer to that friend can help keep you on the straight and narrow. Doing this has been a key way to help me and many others keep the deadly sin of lust at bay.

Committed Christians Often Have the Best Sex

In the last chapter we mentioned the most scientific study to date on the subject of sex in America, which was conducted under the auspices of the University of Chicago. (When it was released in 1993, it made the cover of *Time* magazine.) They found that religion is a *positive* factor in sexual enjoyment, not a negative one. The researchers said, for example, that because of the media: "We see and are told over and over again that all young, healthy Americans were very likely to be having a great deal of sex. . . . Religious conservatives are certainly having less."[8] But in reality they found that those who are committed Christians (my term, not theirs) often have the best sex life. For example, they wrote:

The women with no religious affiliation were somewhat less likely to report that they always had an orgasm, while the conservative Protestant women had the highest rates. . . . The association for women between religious affiliation and orgasms may seem surprising because conservative religious women are so often portrayed as sexually repressed. Perhaps conservative Protestant women firmly believe in the holiness of marriage and of sexuality as an expression of their love for their husbands. In this sense, the findings are consistent with the other findings on sexual satisfaction.[9]

In short, committed Christians, following God's rules, generally have the best sex lives. That's not something you're likely to hear on the evening news.

Conclusion

One day in London many years ago, two earnest seminary students were walking down the streets around the marketplace. One noticed a sign in a window by a rack of clothes. It read: "Slightly soiled—greatly reduced in price." One student said to the other something quite profound related to this issue of purity: "That's it exactly . . . we get soiled by gazing at a vulgar picture, reading a coarse book, or allowing ourselves a little indulgence in dishonest or lustful thoughts; and so when the time comes for our character to be appraised, we are greatly reduced in value. Our purity, our strength is gone. We are just part of parcel of the general, shopworn stock of the world."[10] Thankfully, even if we have fallen in this area and we have been "soiled," there is forgiveness through Christ and there is the strength to change, especially by the renewing of the mind, which comes from focusing on the Scriptures.

chapter 13

Gluttony

I am *in shape—in the shape of a pear!*

—My older brother Rick when he was overweight and out of shape

A man went into a pizza parlor and ordered a medium-sized pizza. When it was ready, the cook asked him if he wanted it cut into four pieces or six pieces. The man thought for a moment and then said, "Cut it into four pieces because I don't think I can eat six."[1] Seriously, for many of us, watching our weight can be an ongoing struggle—especially if we've been watching our weight go up and up.

In fact, a recent poll revealed that now more than half of Americans—54 percent, to be exact—are overweight beyond a level that is "healthy." The journal *Science* reports that in the last two decades the percentage of overweight Americans has increased by approximately one-third. Furthermore, they found that at least a quarter of children today are overweight.[2] Obviously, there can be physiological problems that cause obesity for some.

But for far more Americans, it's a matter of discipline, poor eating habits, and not enough exercise. In short, we're living beyond our seams. Let's begin by looking at what the Bible says about eating and gluttony.

Adam and Eve Sin by Eating

Food was man's first temptation (although the issue boiled down to obedience vs. disobedience). Victor Buono cleverly summed up Genesis:

> Paradise was very nice
> for Adam and his madam
> until they filched the fruit and took the fall.
> They lost their place and fell from grace
> and you can bet we can't forget
> that *eating* is the oldest sin of all.[3]

Did You Know?

54 percent of Americans are now overweight to an unhealthy degree.

Source: *Science.* Reported in Associated Press, 29 May 1998

Esau Satisfies His Stomach

Jacob and Esau, grandsons of Abraham, were twins, but Esau was born first, and therefore was entitled to receive twice the inheritance that his brother would receive. But one day, tired and hungry, Esau traded his inheritance for some red stew. In Genesis 25:29–34 we read:

> Once when Jacob was cooking some stew, Esau
> came in from the open country, famished. He said to

Jacob, "Quick, let me have some of that red stew! I'm famished!" . . .

Jacob replied, "First sell me your birthright."

"Look, I am about to die," Esau said. "What good is the birthright to me?"

But Jacob said, "Swear to me first." So he swore an oath to him, selling his birthright to Jacob.

Then Jacob gave Esau some bread and some lentil stew. He ate and drank, and then got up and left.

So Esau despised his birthright.

Adam and Eve lost paradise; Esau lost his earthly inheritance.

The Israelites Complained About the Lack of Meat

The children of Israel wandering in the wilderness were given manna to eat. They did not have to work to get it because it fell from heaven with the morning dew. All they had to do was gather it up. It looked like white coriander seed and tasted like wafers made with honey (Exod. 16:31) or pastry prepared with oil (Num. 11:8). It could be baked, boiled, ground, beaten, cooked in pans, and made into cakes (Exod. 16:23; Num. 11:8). This miraculous food nourished the Israelites for forty years. But in the beginning, they were not satisfied with it. They were tired of living by bread alone. They yielded to an intense craving for meat and began to complain: "The rabble with them began to crave other food, and again the Israelites started wailing and said, 'If only we had meat

There is something in the red of a raspberry pie that looks as good to a man as the red in a sheep looks to a wolf.

—Edgar Watson Howe,
Sinner Sermons, 1926

to eat! We remember the fish which we ate in Egypt at no cost—also the cucumbers, melons, leeks, onions and garlic. But now we have lost our appetite; we never see anything but this manna!" (Num. 11:4–6).

Their complaining made God so angry that, although He sent them a flock of quail, He also punished their lack of faith and their rebellious spirit. "But while the meat was still between their teeth and before it could be consumed, the anger of the LORD burned against the people, and he struck them with a severe plague. Therefore the place was named Kibroth Hattaavah ["graves of craving"], because there they buried the people who had craved other food" (Num. 11:33–34).

Hopni and Phineas Robbed Meat from God

Eli was a good priest, but his sons were very wicked and did not know the Lord. They had no respect for sacrifices made to God. Flaunting His laws, they would take a meat hook and eat the meat right out of the pot as it was boiling, or, even worse, take the meat before it had been offered in sacrifice. If any worshiper objected (and they had good reason to object), then the brothers would counter: "No, hand it over now; if you don't, I'll take it by force" (1 Sam. 2:16). Because of this, God brought judgment on Eli and his family. Hopni and Phineas were killed by the Philistines at the battle of Shiloh (1 Sam. 4:17), leaving Eli with no descendants, and transferring the priesthood to Samuel. All this, because they stole God's food, and defied His laws.

Jesus, Tempted with Bread

Before the beginning of His ministry, Jesus purified Himself by fasting and praying in the wilderness for forty days. After that He was hungry. Satan tempted Him, saying, "If you are the Son of God, tell these stones to become bread" (Matt. 4:3b). But Jesus successfully resisted the temptation, saying, "It is written: 'Man does not live on bread alone, but on every word that comes from the mouth of God'" (Matt. 4:4).

Jesus Was Accused of Being a Glutton

It's amazing to think that Jesus was actually accused of gluttony. (Somehow I could picture that happening to Buddha, but to Christ?) Luke tells us, "For John the Baptist came neither eating bread nor drinking wine, and you say, 'He has a demon.' The Son of Man came eating and drinking, and you say, 'Here is a glutton and a drunkard, a friend of tax collectors and "sinners"'" (Luke 7:33–34).

Knowing that Jesus passed up the temptation to eat after forty days of fasting, we are astounded to think that anyone would call him a glutton and a drunkard, but that is exactly what His enemies did. They did

> *One thing you can always be sure of— there are more people going on diets tomorrow than are going on diets today.*
>
> —Anonymous

it because it was a terrible insult, and they wanted to say anything that would prejudice the people against Him. When John the Baptist came, he refused to drink strong drink, so his enemies insulted him by saying he had a demon. They said the demon made him sad, that he acted like he was in mourning. When Jesus came, they said just the opposite. Jesus came eating and drinking, and they criticized Him essentially for being too happy. The only thing they wanted to do was criticize both John the Baptist and Jesus.

Why was it such an insult to be called a glutton and a drunkard? The answer lies in Deuteronomy 21:18–21:

> If a man has a stubborn and rebellious son who does
> not obey his father and mother and will not listen to
> them when they discipline him, his father and mother

shall take hold of him and bring him to the elders at the gate of his town. They shall say to the elders, "This son of ours is stubborn and rebellious. He will not obey us. He is a profligate [one who is grossly self-indulgent] and a drunkard." Then all the men of his town shall stone him to death. You must purge the evil from among you. All Israel will hear of it and be afraid.

Matthew Henry notes that this rebellious son is not a child but a grown man, and either his parents have warned him against being a glutton and a drunkard, or he has become a glutton and a drunkard, which has impaired his thinking so that he has become insolent and obstinate.[4]

When I began working on this book, I didn't have a clue that gluttony was sort of a capital crime in Old Testament times. Nor did I realize the significance of the specious charge against Jesus.

Howard Clark Kee said that "more is at stake than relations within the family, however. He [the rebellious son] constitutes a threat to the welfare of the community as a whole."[5]

Other Bible Passages Against Gluttony

- "He who keeps the law is a discerning son, / but a companion of gluttons disgraces his father" (Prov. 28:7).

- "When you sit to dine with a ruler, / note well what is before you, / and put a knife to your throat / if you are given to gluttony. / Do not crave his delicacies, / for that food is deceptive" (Prov. 23:1–3).

- "If you find honey, eat just enough—too much of it, and you will vomit" (Prov. 25:16).

Gluttony a Problem throughout the Ages

In Roman times, there were orgies where people lay on couches to eat. When they ate too much, they could go to special rooms called *vomitoriums* to disgorge, and then come back for more. I have often wondered why *gluttony* would be viewed as one of the seven deadly sins. I think it's quite possible that the medieval marks were resting against the excesses of decadent Rome.

> *It's not the minutes you spend at the table that make you fat, it's the seconds.*
>
> —Anonymous

In some cultures fatness was (is) a sign of wealth because the poor were always scrambling to get enough to eat. In fact, when I was in India in the late 1970s, an Indian friend of mine told me that that was true of their culture.

One Bite Too Much

The American-based organization Overeaters Anonymous disagrees. "OA says that gluttony begins with one bite too much. When we give in to that first compulsive bite, we walk from the protection of our Higher Power into the snare of self-indulgence. Sometimes we are lucky enough to escape the consequences, but usually we are caught in our own trap."[6]

World's Heaviest Humans

Do you know how heavy the heaviest humans are? *The Guinness Book of World Records* lists fifteen men over 880 pounds. They may have medical problems, but they also ate one bite at a time. The heaviest man who ever lived was Jon Brower Minnoch (1941–83). A former taxi driver, he was 6'1" and 1400 pounds, and lived on Bainbridge Island, Washington. In March 1978, he called for a medical rescue, and it took a team of twelve firefighters to carry him on a plank to a ferry boat and then to the University Hospital at Seattle. Dr. Robert Schwartz, the endocrinologist who examined him, estimated his weight at more than 1,400 pounds, a

Mary had a little lamb,
A lobster and some prunes;
A glass of rum, a piece of pie
And then some macaroons.
It made the cafe waiters grin
To see her order so,
And when they carried Mary out
Her face was white as snow.

—Uncle Mat's Magazine
Eleanor Doan, *Speakers Sourcebook II.*

good deal of which was water accumulation due to congestive heart failure. (His actual recorded weight was 975 pounds in September 1976.) It took thirteen attendants to roll him over in his hospital bed. After nearly two years in the hospital on a 1,200-calorie diet, he was discharged weighing 476 pounds. Unfortunately, he gained some weight back. When he died in September 1983, he weighed more than 800 pounds, was rolled to the funeral home in his hospital bed, and was buried in a double-size wooden casket that took up two funeral plots.[7] An extreme case, no doubt. But sometimes the extreme can be a good warning not to let gluttony go unchecked.

Are You a Glutton?

If so far you cannot identify with any of this, nor can you see yourself as a future glutton, consider how the scholastics of the Middle Ages viewed gluttony. For them gluttonous behavior took five forms:

1. Eating too soon
2. Eating too expensively
3. Eating too much

4. Eating too eagerly
5. Eating with too much attention.[8]

Surely we do this quite a bit. Is it any wonder so many of us struggle with being overweight?

We Are a Culture Obsessed with Food

The proof that we are obsessed with food is that obesity is one of the most common health problems in the U.S. It is estimated that 20 to 30 percent of Americans are *seriously* overweight. Even worse, obesity is the number-one health problem of American children. People are said to be obese if they are 20 percent overweight. If a person is more than 30 percent overweight, the medical term is "morbidly obese." Life insurance records indicate that those who are overweight do not live as long as normal people, and that they are prone to high blood pressure, heart disease, stroke, diabetes, varicose veins, and certain forms of cancer.[9]

We glory in our love of food by giving food lovers exotic names. The most discerning is the *epicure*. He is such a connoisseur that he is conscious of much more than just the taste. He wants to know about the source and manner of production. Close behind him is the *gourmet*. His desire is to experience taste and savor it to the fullest. Down another notch is the *gourmand*. He has a healthy appetite for food and drink, and is interested in quantity as well as quality. A *gastronome* is another kind of epicure. His main concern is with ritual and eating the right foods with the right wines. One of my favorite cartoons is of a so-called gastronome asking a wine expert, "What kind of wine goes best with Hamburger Helper?" A *bon vivant* is a gregarious individual who takes a lively pleasure in eating and drinking with others.[10]

No One Wants to Be Called a Glutton

Certainly, no one wants to be called a glutton. A *glutton* is a voracious, hearty eater with an indiscriminate appetite, and according to

Overeaters Anonymous, without any power to stop. Mary Louise Bringle put it this way:

> I remember times when I have been so set on bingeing I have fished for food out of garbage cans. I remember being tempted to steal food from stores, not because I couldn't afford paying for it, but because I was embarrassed for the cashier to see me buying so much snack food. I remember eating food that belonged to the three other women with whom I shared a duplex and rushing to the grocery store to replace it for fear of being discovered. I remember driving miles around Atlanta to go to different franchises of the same fast food establishment because I was embarrassed to buy the number of biscuits I wanted at a single Mrs. Winner's restaurant. I remember eating an entire bag of Pecan Sandies at one sitting, mouthful after frantic mouthful, and feeling my heart begin to pound irregularly. I remember thinking dully, "I'm eating myself into a heart attack; I'm committing a slow form of suicide."[11]

Gluttony Is a Spiritual Problem

Gluttony is no laughing matter. Nor should it be ignored or taken lightly. Gluttony is a spiritual problem. When British Professor John Garrow said, "I would not mind being around hyperactive [gluttons] so long as their other motives were purged of the other deadly sins,"[12] he was imagining an impossible situation. People usually become gluttons because they have other hurts, problems, or sins they do not want to face. In the case of the son in Deuteronomy 21, he was rebellious and obstinate. Scripture tells us that rebellion is like the sin of witchcraft (1 Sam. 15:23, NKJV). Rebellious people are selfish and irresponsible. Gluttons are often irresponsible about food. They can always find reasons for why they eat. When they feel frustrated, overwhelmed, ashamed, afraid, full of self-pity, bored, nervous, lonely, angry, tired, or when they feel happy and want to celebrate, they turn to food rather than God. This is wrong. Jesus said, "Man does not live on bread alone, but on every word that comes from the mouth of God" (Matt. 4:4).

Ironically, though gluttony is a spiritual problem, many Christians have a big problem in this area. For example, at the 1997 annual Southern Baptist Convention, a fellow Baptist and trainer, Ray Furr, found that 60 percent of those surveyed were over-weight.[13] Furr stated: "If you are going to act like God's servant, you need to look like one."[14]

Conclusion

The good news is, despite a lifetime of bad habits in the realm of eating, through Christ we can regain new and improved ways of approaching food. A friend of ours from church tells of her own struggle with "the battle of the bulge." With her insightful words, we close out this chapter:

> I have struggled with gluttony all my life. I was raised in a home where food was plentiful and there were no restrictions about eating between meals. Whenever I did not feel well physically or was anxious about something, my first thought was "If I eat something, maybe I'll feel better." Today I am recovering from gluttony through a spiritual program. It is possible. If gluttony is your "big battle," do not despair. There are successful strategies that work. A Bible verse that I have meditated on a lot is Galatians 2:20: "I have been crucified with Christ and I no longer live, but Christ lives in me. The life I live in the body, I live by faith in the son of God, who loved me and gave Himself for me." To me

> *Let Christ stay throughout the meal. Don't dismiss Him with the blessing.*
>
> —Eleanor Doan

this verse means there are two realities: My past failures and God's unconditional love. If I forget that I have been crucified with Christ, then I will concentrate on my failures. If I remember I have been crucified with Christ, then I will concentrate on His unconditional love for me.[15]

At last check, our friend had lost more than twenty pounds or so and has been keeping if off consistently.

chapter 14

Self-Control

Arteriosclerosis can truthfully be called "everyone's disease."

—Dr. S. I. McMillen and David Stern

"There is no love sincerer than the love of food,"[1] and because of that many of us play food games. Consider this: An overweight man was in the habit of going to a bakery on his way to work to pick up goodies for the staff coffee break. He stopped doing it when he went on a diet, and the staff understood. But one day, while he was running errands for the office, he had to drive by the bakery and he said to himself, "Maybe God wants me to stop and pick up some goodies for the office." So he told God, "I will stop only if You make a parking place available right in front of the bakery." And sure enough, there it was—on his eighth trip around the block.[2]

Self-control is the ultimate fruit of the Spirit, the one listed last. It is not only a gift, it is also a character trait that has to be developed through self-denial. The virtue of self-control is essential for the Christian walk. A person who has a problem with overindulgence when it comes to food or alcohol, or any other of God's gifts, often has a deep-seated problem with self-control in other areas of life as well. Gluttony is a symptom of overindulgence and lack of control.

> *Like a city whose walls are broken down, is a man who lacks self-control.*
>
> —Proverbs 25:28

I often think of a cartoon I saw where a man in a restaurant was talking to the waitress. He said, "If I order pie, don't bring it."

Lack of Self-Control Is Costly

Americans spend some $33 billion a year on weight-loss products—$1.3 billion is spent on appetite suppressants alone. Medically supervised fasting plans can reduce your bank account by $2,065 for 26 weeks; four or five sessions at a hospital workshop, $250; diet pills, meal replacements and other self-help solutions, $220–$390.[3]

Lack of Self-Control Is Deadly

Obesity is a killer. For persons between 45 and 50, here is how the death rate increases as overweight pounds increase: 10 lbs. - 8 percent, 20 lbs. - 18 percent, 30 lbs. - 28 percent, 40 lbs. - 45 percent, 50 lbs. - 56 percent, 60 lbs. - 67 percent, 70 lbs. - 81 percent, 90 lbs. - 116 percent.[4] One and a half million Americans have heart attacks every year, and over one-third of them die. If every American were at his optimum weight, we would see an astounding decrease. Heart attacks would decrease 25 percent, strokes and heart failure, over 30 percent.[5]

Being Rich and Famous Does Not Help

Many Hollywood stars battle constantly to keep their weight down. These include Elizabeth Taylor, Susan Ruttan, Jack Nicholson, Roseanne, Tom Arnold, comedian Louie Anderson, Dom DeLuise, and Oprah Winfrey.[6] How celebrities control their weight is of such great interest to Americans that it is constantly in the news. In their March 3, 1998 issue, *People Magazine* ran an excerpt from the memoirs of Delta Burke of TV's *Designing Women,* entitled *Delta Style: Eve Wasn't a Size 6 (and Neither Am I),*[7] as well as an article about Susan Estrich, feminist, attorney, and first woman to manage a presidential campaign, who lost forty pounds in five months and has become a diet guru with her book, *Making a Case for Yourself: A Diet Book for Smart Women.*[8] Rush Limbaugh at last check has lost more than sixty pounds in the last several months. In some cases, though, being overweight was fatal to celebs. John Candy died at an early age, and Mamma Cass Elliott of the Mamas and the Papas died with a fork in her mouth.

God's Rules for Eating

Whether we like it or not, there have always been rules for eating, and we need them. In the beginning we were all vegetarians. In Genesis 1:29, we read, "I give you every seed-bearing plant on the face of the whole earth and every tree that has fruit with seed in it." God was generous with the food He supplied (with the obvious restriction of the tree of the knowledge of good and evil). God also expects us to be thankful for our food. "When you have eaten and are satisfied, praise the LORD your God for the good land he has given you" (Deut. 8:10).

As time went on, God's people became meat eaters, and God laid down some rules about which animals they could eat and which animals were forbidden (Lev. 11; Deut. 14). He also gave strict instructions about the parts of the animals they were allowed to eat. Fat and blood were forbidden (Lev. 7:23–25).

Aside from the forbidden foods and the parts of animals that were not allowed, God had no diet or food plan that He commanded the people to follow. Nor were they obsessed with dieting as we are today. There are probably two reasons for this. First, because the people had to walk everywhere, they got plenty of exercise. Second, because they were religious, they practiced fasting.

Biblical Fasting

All of the Israelites were supposed to fast one day a year on the Day of Atonement (Num. 29:7–35; Lev. 23:26–32). Fasting meant they could not eat or drink anything from sundown to sundown, and they were to humble themselves prayerfully before the Lord with sorrow and repentance. However, fasting was not limited to this day only. A king could call for a national day of prayer and fasting if the country were in danger of war or destruction. Queen Esther asked her people to fast for three days because Haman wanted to kill them all (Esther 4:16). After the destruction of Jerusalem in 587 B.C., four fast days were proclaimed, one each in the fourth, fifth, seventh, and tenth months (Zech. 8:19). People also fasted privately when they were oppressed with cares. King David fasted when his child was sick (2 Sam. 12:16–23). Those who fasted the longest in the Bible were Jesus (Matt. 4:2), Moses (Exod. 34:28), and Elijah (1 Kings 19:8). They each fasted forty days and forty nights. The Pharisees who considered themselves to be extremely religious fasted two days a week. When the Pharisees criticized Jesus' disciples for not fasting, Jesus responded, "How can the guests of the bridegroom fast while he is with them? They cannot, so long as they have him with them. But the time will come when the bridegroom will be taken away from them, and on that day they will fast" (Mark 2:19–20). Jesus did not condemn fasting, but he believed it should not be ostentatious. "When you fast, do not look somber as the hypocrites do, for they disfigure their faces to show men they are fasting. I tell you the truth, they have received their reward in full. But when you fast, put oil on your head and wash your face, so that it will not be obvious to men that you are fasting, but only to your Father, who is unseen; and your Father, who sees what is done in secret, will reward you" (Matt. 6:16–18). Note that Jesus didn't say "if you fast," but rather "when you fast." Surely this implies that He intends us to fast sometimes. Fasting is a biblical way of learning self-control, but that is a side blessing. The purpose of fasting is prayer and humble repentance.

Fasting in the Christian Church

Jewish Christians followed the practice of fasting on Monday and Thursday until the end of the first century, when Wednesday and Friday were observed. In the second century, two intensive fast days were observed in preparation for Easter. In the fourth century the two fast days were extended into the forty days of Lent. During the Middle Ages, the Catholic Church added fast days on Wednesday, Friday, and Saturday, following the first Sunday of Lent, Pentecost, September 14, and December 13.[9] The Protestant Reformation rejected fasting because they thought it was done for the wrong reasons. They felt it was more legalistic than spiritual and that it was done to get things from God or as a substitute for genuine repentance. In the twentieth century the Catholic Church modified fasting through Vatican II, which took place in the 1960s. Their fasting now consists of a "love your neighbor approach," where you eat a simple meal, and give the money you would have spent on yourself to the poor.

One church today that actively practices fasting is the Russian Orthodox. Its calendar contains four significant fasts: Lent, seven weeks; the Assumption, two weeks; the Christmas fast, forty days; Petrovsky, one to six weeks. Additionally, there are several one-day fasts. Apart from these, believers fast regularly on Wednesday and Friday.[10]

Generally practicing fasts from time to time is good both for the soul and the body.

Christian Dieting:
A Twentieth-Century Phenomenon

From fasting, we shift to dieting. The first person to kick off the Christian dieting movement was Dr. Charles Shedd with his *Pray Your Weight Away* (1957). Shedd believed that being fat was a sin. He dished out such statement as, "When God first dreamed you into creation, there weren't 100 extra pounds hanging around your belt." or "We fatties are the only people on earth who can weigh our sins."[11] As time has gone by, the Christian fitness gurus have shifted the focus from sin to addiction, treating overeaters less like reprobates and more like victims. Their idea is not so much that fat people offend God but that they need help in battling an obsession with food.

The Best-Selling Christian
Weight-Loss Programs

If you are looking for a Christian weight-loss program, here are the three best-selling ones in 1998:

1. *Free to be Thin* by Neva Coyle and Marie Chapin.[12] Neva Coyle is the founder of Overeaters Victorious. Hers is a thirteen-week plan that is billed as a ministry to overweight people and overeaters. It includes positive affirmations, such as "Today, I walk in victory. Today I am totally victorious over food. I do not abuse it or use it for satisfaction, reward or emotional outlet. I do not express my anger or frustration by overeating. Jesus satisfies me."[13]

2. *First Place* by Carole Lewis with Terry Whalin.[14] Her diet is approved by the American Diabetic Association and is built on nine "commitments": (1) regular attendance at group meetings, (2) prayer, (3) Bible reading, (4) Scripture memory, (5) Bible study, (6) live it (not die-it), (7) fact sheet, (8) daily phone calls, and (9) exercise.[15]

3. *The Weigh Down Diet* by Gwen Shamblin.[16] This diet is currently in ten thousand churches nationwide. Her accompanying exercise video *Praise Aerobics* has sold over fifty thousand copies. Her thirteen-week program requires no charts or calorie counting. Instead, she advocates not eating if you are not hungry, and she will teach you how to stop after you have eaten half a candy bar.

Other effective diets include fasting for weight loss (which is recommended only with great caution) and the "Hallelujah Diet," which is a plant-based food plan involving no animal or dairy products.[17]

> *Out of 100 participating nations of the world, America was the healthiest in 1900. In 1920, we dropped to the second healthiest nation. During World War II, we went back to number one—that's when sugar and meat were hard to get and family vegetable gardens were common. In 1978, we dropped to 79th. In 1980, we were 95th. Today we are number 100 on the list.*
>
> —The U.S. Public Health Service

Self-Control for Food Addicts Is Possible

All of the programs mentioned so far work well for some people. But what if you have an eating disorder? Don't despair. There is a wonderful, Christ-centered twelve-step program that can help. It is called *Conquering Eating Disorders*. The book by the same name is actually a workbook that allows you to work through the twelve steps at your own pace.[18] The first thing it does is to help you determine which kind of eating disorder you have by asking a series of questions. There are four kinds of eating disorders: anorexia, bulimia, compulsive overeating, and pica.[19] The

> ## How to Spell Success with Food
>
> Set aside time each day to be alone with God.
>
> Understand we have no strength on our own, but depend on God.
>
> Call on God when fear overtakes you.
>
> Call a [friend] for support.
>
> Enjoy your journey.
>
> Stay in God's Word.
>
> Seek to love more today than yesterday.
>
> —Carole Lewis with Terry Whalin, *First Place.*

workbook deals with the first three. (It does not deal with pica because pica is an eating disorder in which children eat dirt and bugs.) In addition to the workbook, there are weekly meetings in which participants, who have weighed and measured their food, turn in a log sheet of what they ate during the past week. During the week they are required to call their food sponsor and three other persons every day. They are only allowed to weigh themselves once a month in private. They are given Bible verses to memorize.

This program has a tremendous success rate. Mary Kay Tortoriello, a recovering food addict and food addictions counselor lost over sixty pounds and has kept it off for nine years. She considers this not to be a diet but a way of life to honor Christ. As stated in Romans 12:1, "Therefore, I urge you, brothers, in view of God's mercy, to offer your bodies as living sacrifices, holy and pleasing to God—that is your spiritual act of worship."

Additionally, she is a biblical counselor and an adjunct instructor at South Florida Bible College. She has appeared on various Christian talk shows, including my radio show on several occasions, speaking on conquering eating disorders and breaking the cycle of hurtful family relationships.

A person who thinks he has a serious (e.g., anorexia or bulimia) eating disorder should get professional help from an eating disorder therapist, because, in order to recover, he needs an assessment and psychological testing.[20]

Conclusion

You do not have to be like a city whose walls are broken down (which is the way the Bible describes someone without self-control (Prov. 25:28)). You can handle your food wisely and well if you follow two principles: surrender and obedience. I close with some additional encouraging words from Mary Kay Tortoriello:

If you want to be successful in this program, you need to be patient and brave to stay in the program. Remember you have choices. . . . God wants to make a covenant with you (Deuteronomy 29:1) . . . God will rejoice if you obey the commandments written in this book of the law and if you turn to the Lord your God with all your hearts and souls. Obeying these commandments is not beyond your reach; for these laws are not in the heavens so distant that you can't hear and obey them, and with no one to bring them down to you; nor are they beyond the ocean, so far that no one can bring you the message; but they are very close at hand—in your hearts and on your lips so that you can obey them. . . .

The Israelites were on the verge of entering the Promised Land. (Deuteronomy 31:3). They needed a fresh reminder of God's strength and a promise of victory. Some may have been putting their confidence in

Joshua. Others may have been depending on the strength of their armies. But no matter how strong we are or how strong our leaders might be, victory comes from God alone. Some enemies are too great for us. Our personal resources of support groups, though helpful, will never be adequate to help us gain victory over our dependencies. We must learn to trust God alone, for he is greater than any of the enemies we might face.[21]

Food addictions are chronic, progressive, and potentially fatal. They can be just as destructive as chemical dependency, and their emotional damage leads to isolation, depression, and thoughts of suicide. Women are ten times more susceptible to eating disorders than men. However, men are becoming more open about it and need support and encouragement. If you are a normal eater, you eat what you want when you want, know when you are full, and are able to stop, but if you have an eating disorder, you cannot do any of these things.

—Mary Kay Tortoriello

chapter 15

Sloth

*God sells us all things
at the price of labor.*

—Leonardo da Vinci

Did you ever hear about the patient who went for a very thorough examination by a doctor? The patient said that he wanted the doctor to be honest and frank about what was wrong with him. The doctor asked him if he was quite sure about this. The patient replied in the affirmative. "Well," said the doctor, "there isn't a thing in the world wrong with you, except that *you are just plain lazy!*" The patient answered, "Okay, doc. Now give me the medical term for it so I can tell my wife!"[1]

In this chapter we want to explore the deadly sin of sloth—at the workplace (which is increasingly becoming more common), in the family setting, and in the spiritual realm. Deep down, many of us are quite lazy, or at least we have the natural bent toward sloth. It's interesting that most of the other deadly sins involve some act of commission; they involve sinning by thought, word, or deed.

But with the sin of sloth, the sin boils down to what we *don't* do. As has been said so often before: "The road to hell is paved with good intentions."

> *Life is a leaf of white paper*
> *Whereon each of us may write*
> *His word or two, and then comes night.*
> *Greatly begin! Though thou have time*
> *But for a line, be that sublime,*
> *Not failure, but low aim, is crime.*
>
> —Walter B. Knight

Thoughts on Life's Difficulties

Life this side of the fall is not easy nor is work. But to the slothful, it would seem that *any* work is a strain.

The earth is under a curse, and we experience that curse in one way or another each day. God declared to Adam in judgment:

"Cursed is the ground because of you;
through painful toil you will eat of it
all the days of your life.
It will produce thorns and thistles for you,
and you will eat the plants of the field.
By the sweat of your brow
you will eat your food" (Gen. 3:17–19).

Ecclesiastes describes a bleak picture of man's daily existence as he toils every day under the sun in order to enjoy for a moment fleeting pleasures.

A bumper sticker declares the daily grind of many people: "I owe, I owe, so off to work I go!"

Some excuse their laziness because of the difficulties we all face. Consider the average day for many people these stressful

> *"I haven't time!" These idle words*
> *Are not exactly true,*
> *Because I always find the time*
> *For things I want to do.*
>
> —Herbert V. Prochnow and Herbert V. Prochnow, Jr., eds,
> *The Toastmaster's Treasure Chest*

days: You wake up early in the morning, when you'd rather sleep in. You get ready for work. You rush off to work in bumper-to-bumper traffic. You find pressures on the job from the minute you enter the office until the time you leave. Then you fight rush-hour traffic. You get home and are so mentally fatigued that you don't want to do anything but watch TV, which can sometimes be even more mentally fatiguing. Finally, you go to bed exhausted. And then the alarm rings, and it's already another day. Though life can be hard for all of us, those who are slothful will find that it's made

> *No man is born into the world whose work is*
> *not born with him. There is always work,*
> *and tools to work with, for those who will*
> *work. Blessed be the thorny hands of toil.*
>
> —James Russell Lowell

even harder by their laziness. I know a man who is virtually allergic to work. He seems to be constantly looking for employment. But then when he gets it, he can't seem to keep it for long either because of laziness on the job reflected in poor performance or even because of the lack of basics in hygiene. I once asked him where he wanted to be five years from now. His immediate answer—he didn't even have to think about it—was, "I want to be rich!" It's tragic because he's not doing the things that could lead him to his goal. Ironically, he's a professing Christian. But there are several indicators, including his poor work ethic, that would seem to demonstrate that he's generally not walking with the Lord.

Sloth in the Ancient World

We don't necessarily think of ancient man as being lazy. But I think it's fair to say that ancient *wealthy* man was. The Greeks and the Romans used their slaves to do their hard work. Larry Burkett pointed out, "The Greeks degraded into a nation of idle talkers who were easily overrun by the Romans."[2] In our book, *What If Jesus Had Never Been Born?* Dr. Kennedy and I pointed out:

Prior to Christ, the nations of antiquity despised honest work and consigned it to slaves . . . three-quarters of Athens and half of the Roman empire were made up of slaves. We get a taste of how "gentlemen" did no labor in ancient Greece in Acts 17, when Paul visited the Athenians to spread the gospel there. "For all the Athenians and the foreigners who were there spent their time in nothing else but either to tell or to hear some new thing" (Acts 17:21, NKJV).

> *The person who takes his time often takes yours too.*
>
> —Anonymous

But Jesus revolutionized labor. By picking up the saw, the hammer and the plane, he imbued labor with a new dignity. Over the centuries, where the gospel worked its way into and throughout a land, it translated the slaves and serfs into people of the working

> *Laziness travels so slowly that poverty soon overtakes him.*
>
> —Jo Petty

classes. Without work, it is impossible for any human being to fulfill the probation that God has given him in this life.[3]

Glued to the Television Set

I think an area of sloth in our time is the amount of time we spend watching television. Did God put us on the earth so that we'd keep up with all the latest on the prime-time schedule? I don't think so. The statistics on American TV viewing are discouraging. According to a 1996 source, the average American adult views television for twenty-six hours a week; the average child for twenty-three hours a week.[4] Twenty-six hours a week adds up to more than 1,300 hours a year.

Did you know?

Not surprisingly, a study showed that many CEOs of Fortune 500 companies spend precious little time watching TV. In fact, 81 percent of them watch less than one hour of television per day. That's significantly lower than the national average!

—D. James Kennedy with Jerry Newcombe,
The Gates of Hell Shall Not Prevail

Often you'll hear the excuse, "Oh, there just isn't enough time!" (For example, try getting volunteers at your church for evangelism.) Yet we have enough time to watch so much TV? I love the old quip from Groucho Marx when he said, "I find TV very educating. Every time somebody turns on the set I go into the other room and read a book."[5]

Robin MacNeil, formerly of the acclaimed *MacNeil-Lehrer News Hour* on PBS, demonstrated the important opportunity losses associated with spending so much time viewing television:

It is difficult to escape the influences of television. If you fit the statistical averages, by the age of 20 you will have been exposed to at least 20,000 hours of television. You can add 10,000 hours for each decade you have lived after the age of 20. The only things Americans do more than watch TV is sleep.

Calculate for a moment what could be done with even a part of those hours. Five thousand hours, I am told, are what a typical college undergraduate spends working on a bachelor's degree. In 10,000 hours you could have learned enough to become an astronomer or engineer. You could have learned several languages fluently. If it appealed to you, you could be reading Homer in the original Greek or Dostoyevsky in Russian. If it didn't, you could have walked around the world and written a book about it.

> *It has been said that success is a ladder which cannot be climbed with our hands in our pockets.*
>
> —Anonymous

The trouble with television is that it discourages concentration. Almost anything interesting and rewarding in life requires some constructive, consistently applied effort. The dullest, the least gifted of us can achieve things that seem miraculous to those who never concentrate on anything.[6]

Hearing that offends me so much I want to grab the clicker and switch over to the next channel.

Long before the invention of television, D. L. Moody once said, "Now, if you want to be a useful, happy Christian, just get to work and do not go to sleep. We have enough of sleepy Christians. If a church has nothing for you to do, do not go into it. Find some church where you can find something to do. If you want to be a healthy Christian you have got to work."[7] He also observed that "many people are working and working, like children on a rocking horse—it is a beautiful motion, but there is no progress."[8]

Robert G. Lee once pointed out how important it is to not squander the precious commodity of time:

> If you had a bank that credited your account each morning with $86,400, that carried no balance from day to day, allowed you to keep no cash in your account, and finally every evening canceled whatever part of the amount you had failed to use during the day, what would you do? Draw out every cent—of course! Well, you have such a bank and its name is "Time." Every morning it credits you with 86,400 seconds. Every night it rules off—as lost—whatever of this you have failed to invest to good purpose. It carries no balances. It allows no balances. It allows no overdrafts. Each day the bank named "Time" opens a new account with you. Each night it burns to records of the day. If you fail to use the day's deposits the loss is yours.[9]

What a great way of thinking about it. What happens so often though is we tend to think along the lines, "I have so many days, weeks, months, and years ahead," so we procrastinate over things that are truly important. We let things slide. Sloth is the least difficult of all the seven deadly sins to commit. No effort at all. Contrast the deadly sin of sloth with the deadly sin of gluttony in one statement of Proverbs: "The sluggard is so lazy he won't even bring the fork to his mouth!" (paraphrase of Prov. 19:24). Hey, maybe that's the solution to overcoming gluttony.

Sloth Among Employees

Nowadays a good employee is generally hard to find. Talk to anyone who runs a small business and ask her what's the single most difficult aspect of the company. Often that answer boils down to getting good, honest, and reliable employees. Because of the breakdown of character in our time—from high levels on down—many employees are unreliable. They pad their resumés. They use drugs. They steal at the office—if not material things, then they steal time. People say "character doesn't matter." In response to that Bill Bennett said, "Anybody who's ever had to hire a baby-sitter knows that character matters."[10]

Consider these statistics on time theft in the workplace from more than a decade ago. Generally, things have gotten worse in our time. A South Florida newspaper reported, "The average employee 'steals' more than six weeks a year from his company, according to the results of a survey conducted by an executive recruiting firm. The survey showed that time theft added up to about $150 billion in 1984, and cost companies more than all other crimes, including pilfering, insurance fraud, kickbacks, and embezzlement."[11]

Another study found virtually the same results. They reported: 'Persistent theft of on-the-job time can devastate a company,' said personnel expert Robert Half of Palm Beach. Half, who annually surveys business time theft, said it cuts into productivity levels and, consequently, often drives up overtime expenses. 'The problem has reached such proportions,' he said, 'that employers will record $170 billion in time-theft losses this year.'"[12] Furthermore, in yet another study, 33 percent of American "workers" have confessed to researchers that they have phoned in sick—when they really weren't.[13] All of these are symptoms of the deadly sin of sloth.

I think it's interesting to note that the Bible gave an apt description—more than three thousand years ago—of the slothful employee and the impact he has on his boss. Solomon wrote: "As vinegar to the teeth and smoke to the eyes, so is a sluggard to those who send him" (Prov. 10:26).

Several years ago Chuck Colson and pharmaceutical magnate Jack Eckerd joined together to write the sobering book *Why America Doesn't Work*. It documents the slipshod nature of some of our work these days: "In most consumer ratings, American products consistently slip behind foreign competitors, and a recent study concluded that in 1990 the United States, alone among the seven great industrial nations of the world, suffered an actual decline in its real standard of living."[14]

I'm reminded of my parents and their toaster. When they wed in 1948, they received a new toaster as a wedding gift. It worked well for years. Finally, after daily use for twenty years, it broke. They then bought a new one. It lasted about a year. Then they bought another one. It lasted about a year or two. It seemed like they went through an annual ritual of buying a new toaster. It may be because of "planned obsolescence," where the manufacturers build the products in such a way that they will only last for so long, so they'll have repeat business every year or two. But it's disturbing to think that they would do that on purpose.

> *As American productivity, once the exuberant engine of national wealth, has dipped to an embarrassingly uncompetitive low, Americans have shaken their heads: the country's old work ethic is dead.*
>
> —Lance Morrow

Colson and Eckerd pointed out that part of the problem with the decline in American workmanship is the disparity between rewards and salaries for employers vs. employees: "A recent survey found that 43 percent of all workers could be classed as cynical. They don't trust management or their coworkers; they don't think their pay is fair or that they have a fair shot at advancement; they don't believe management listens to them or values what they do on their jobs."[15] This in turn leads to a significant decline in productivity. The Golden Rule has too often been turned to lead. Or worse: the other golden rule (whoever has the gold makes the rules) is the one put into practice.

Spiritual Sloth

Each day more than fifty million Americans buy a meal at a fast-food restaurant. In our culture, where everything is convenient, where we have microwave ovens and fast food, we think and talk sometimes as if holiness is instant. As Jay Adams put it, "You may have sought and tried to obtain instant godliness. There is no such thing. . . . We want somebody to give us three easy steps to godliness, and we'll take them next Friday and be godly. The trouble is godliness doesn't come that way."[16] Growth of any kind, spiritual or otherwise, is not instant. Maturity does not occur overnight.

Have you ever noticed how many people claim they want to know God's will? They go into contortions trying to find what "God's will" is for them, but they don't obey the *simple* things that He's clearly commanded, such as, "Go and be my witnesses" or to read His Word or to spend time in prayer or feed the hungry and visit the sick. Until we obey such basics that He has clearly revealed, we can honestly question how sincere our desire is to know God's will.

Why is the Church not having a stronger impact on our world? I believe that part of the reason boils down to spiritual sloth. We're lazy. David Watson wrote:

With such numerical strength, such a relevant message, and such spiritual power, why is the Christian church, especially in the West so comparatively ineffective? . . . Why is the church in the West in such sharp decline compared with the church in the poverty-stricken countries of the world? . . .

> *If you want your dreams to come true, don't oversleep.*
>
> —Paul Lee Tan

Why? Christians in the West have largely neglected what it means to be disciples of Christ. The vast majority of western Christians—church members, pew fillers, hymn-singers, sermon-tasters, bible-readers, even born-again-believers or spirit-filled-charismatics, are not true disciples of Jesus. If we were willing to become disciples, the church in the West would be transformed, and the impact on society would be staggering. And this is no idle claim. In the first century, a tiny handful of inexperienced, timid disciples initiated, in the power of the Spirit, the greatest spiritual revolution the world has ever known.[17]

My fellow "pew fillers," it's time to take spiritual sloth more seriously. After all, what was the sin of the third man in the parable of the talents—the third servant who failed to show any results to his master after having been entrusted with one talent? His sin was sloth.

It is said of Abraham Lincoln that he could get a large number of men who were "willing to shed their last drop of blood." However, he could get few men who were willing to shed their first drop.[18] Thus we should despise not small beginnings. We should be faithful with what we do have and not worry about what we don't have.

In contrast to spiritual sloth, consider the example of one of the greatest missionaries of all time, the legendary David Livingstone. He plodded along into the interior or unchartered territory in Africa for the gospel's sake. Here's what he wrote in his diary:

I place no value on anything I have or may possess, except in relation to the kingdom of Christ. If anything will advance the interests of the kingdom, it shall be given away or kept, only as by giving or keeping it I shall promote the glory of Him to whom I owe all my hopes in time and eternity.[19]

In the face of all manner of obstacles, including a vicious lion attack, the man risked it all to open up closed territory for Jesus' sake. Here is the antithesis of spiritual sloth.

Conclusion

The apostle who accomplished incredible things for the kingdom of God said, "I can do all things through Christ who strengthens me" (Phil. 4:13, NKJV). My mom often says, "God and I can do anything God can do alone." Truths like these are a sure antidote to sloth. What do we do when we know that there are tasks waiting for us, and we feel like pressing the "delete" and "escape" buttons? Or we feel like hitting the clicker like Mr. Chance in the Peter Sellers movie *Being There* to escape ugly realities by somehow changing the channel on life. What do we do when we know what we have to do and the temptation to skip it is so strong—perhaps because it all seems so overwhelming? We just have to remember God has helped us make it through the day before, and He'll help us make it through this day as well. Through His help we can be more productive than ever before.

chapter 16

Diligence

*Excellence in all things,
and all things to God's glory.*

—Motto of Coral Ridge Presbyterian Church,
Ft. Lauderdale, FL

Paul Harvey tells of an intriguing story of a young author named John Toole who began writing a novel when he was a young man. He finished it in the 1960s when he got out of the army. But he was dismayed to find no one interested in publishing his book. Says Harvey, "One by one the publishers said: 'Thanks, but there is no present market' or simply 'Thanks but no thanks.'"[1]

Meanwhile, John's mother was very interested in her son's book, and she saw greater potential in it than he did. Thelma Toole insisted that her son keep trying to publish his novel. But one day in 1969, after eight publishers turned him down, he quit trying. "What's the use?" But his mother didn't quit trying. One day she finally found a publisher for her son's novel. And the book, *Confederacy of Dunces,* became a best-seller on several lists. It even won the 1981 Pulitzer Prize for fiction. Only it was *Thelma*

194

Toole who accepted the prize because back in 1969, faced with repeated rejections, John Toole had shot himself, ending his life at the age of thirty-two. He hadn't learned the profound truth that comes from a country parson named Frank Clark: "A lot of impulsive mistakes are made by people who simply aren't willing to be bored a little longer."[2]

> *Service is the rent we pay for space we occupy.*
>
> —Anonymous

Many times the difference between success and failure is trying just a little bit more. It's persevering. I love the quote attributed to Mother Teresa: "God doesn't call us to be successful; He calls us to be faithful." In this chapter, we will look at diligence, the antithesis of the deadly sin of sloth.

Bored a Little Longer

W. C. Fields once said, "If at first you don't succeed, try again. If it doesn't work the second time, quit! No use being a _____ fool about it." And yet this is the same W. C. Fields who practiced to all hours of the night to improve his act! He began his career as a juggler. Working in Vaudeville, he would often return to his room late at night, and he stood beside his bed and tossed objects into the air literally until he dropped, and he slept the night through without even extinguishing the light.

> *Lost yesterday, somewhere between sunrise and sunset, two golden hours, each set with sixty diamond minutes. No reward is offered, for they are gone forever.*
>
> —Horace Mann

Most things of lasting value don't come instantly. Success generally doesn't. Good, healthy relationships don't. Good reputations don't. All of these come from clarified objectives, hard work, and persistence—and the willingness to stay bored a little longer.

A study in *Inc.* magazine many years ago researched a large number of millionaires. And they discovered that the profile of the average millionaire was a man, sixty-five years of age, who worked sixty hours a week and had been at the same profession, doing basically the same thing, for a few decades. In short, here was a group who learned the lesson of "being bored a little longer."

Faithful in the Little Things

About a decade ago, I (Jerry) was going through a low period in my life, in my career. I was frustrated with the position I had as a researcher and writer for a TV ministry, and although it's a very reputable TV outreach, I was underemployed, very bored, and constantly looking for other positions. At the time, I was doing a good job, by *their* standards. But not by *mine.* I knew I was capable of accomplishing a lot more in that particular outlet. But one day in my prayer time, one passage of Scripture grabbed my attention. In one of the parables, a master commends his productive servant and says, "Well done, good and faithful servant! You have been faithful with a few things; I will put you in charge of many things" (Matt. 25:21). And this unsettling thought gripped me: "Jerry, you want to move on to a better position, but have you been *faithful* with the few things you *have* been entrusted? Why should you be given bigger responsibilities if you're not faithfully discharging the ones you already have before you?" That question

> *Some people fail to recognize opportunity because it so often comes to them in overalls and looks like work.*
>
> —Anonymous

rigorously shook me because I was not being faithful in my job. I wasn't focusing my energies. So by God's grace, I became more productive and worked toward accomplishing more. I started to give my boss 150 percent instead of 75 percent. Not too long after that, an opportunity opened up for me to work on one project as a producer—the very position I had wanted. This was my chance to prove myself, and I went after it with all my heart—working many late nights and doing a lot of unpaid work to shine in this area. And it paid off. The documentary I coproduced generated a record high response among our viewers. And not long after that, I was officially promoted to the position of producer.

> *The world cannot always understand one's profession of faith, but it can understand service.*
>
> —Ian Maclaren

Wherever we are in life, in our careers, in our families and relationships, in our spiritual lives, there is an abundance of opportunities all around us; if we could just learn to be faithful in the little things. If we could just develop the patience to be bored a little longer.

I love the Bible verse from Ecclesiastes, which says, "Whatever your hand finds to do, do it with all your might" (9:10).

What task lies before you at this point in your life? What opportunity lies before you? Are you being faithful in the few things entrusted in your care? If not, what could you do differently in order to do so?

Mark of Excellence

There's a foreign car that's made so well that each worker puts his initials on the auto's part that he is responsible for producing. This is a stamp of pride (self-respect) in the quality of the workmanship for each particular piece in the car. The quality of the car makes it one of the most expensive on the highway and also one of the most enduring. Each employee works hard, and the result is good craftsmanship.

Diligence has always been a hallmark of God's obedient people. Work is good. Before the fall "God took the man and put him in the Garden of Eden to work it and take care of it" (Gen. 2:15). But after the fall the very ground was cursed, and labor was difficult from then on. We earn our daily bread by the sweat of our brow, but that doesn't mean it isn't good.

The rules that govern work and rest go all the way back to Creation. When God rested on the seventh day, He established a six-day work week. When God gave the commandments to Moses, he referred back to Creation: "Remember the Sabbath day by keeping it holy. Six days you shall labor and do all your work" (Exod. 20:8–9). This commandment is not only about keeping the Sabbath; it also implies that we will work the other six days.

The Book of Proverbs has much to say about sloth and diligence:

- "Lazy hands make a man poor, / but diligent hands bring wealth. / He who gathers crops in summer is a wise son, / but he who sleeps during harvest is a disgraceful son" (Prov. 10:4–5).
- "Diligent hands will rule, / but laziness ends in slave labor" (Prov. 12:24).
- "The sluggard craves and gets nothing, / but the desires of the diligent are fully satisfied" (Prov. 13:4).
- "The plans of the diligent lead to profit / as surely as haste leads to poverty" (Prov. 21:5).

These gems from Proverbs are general principles and not specific promises. If you are diligent, it usually follows that you will prosper.

Retirement?

Several years ago Billy Graham was asked his opinions about retirement. He answered, "I don't think that I can find anybody in the Bible that retired." At the time he said this he was seventy-three![3]

This, of course, doesn't mean that the same principle applies to everybody or that you're a bad Christian if you ultimately retire. But for himself, he has chosen to persevere diligently until the Lord calls him home. To him diligence demands persevering despite the obstacles of age and disease.

> *The church is a workshop, not a dormitory;*
> *and every Christian man and woman is*
> *bound to help in the common cause.*
>
> —Alexander MacLaren

Lack of Focus

Sometimes a lack of focus can be a serious impediment to diligence. Rather than "staying bored a little longer," we can end up flitting to one thing and then another, never quite accomplishing anything of substance. Here's an example of an unfocused life—despite a potential with great promise. It comes from Gordon MacDonald as he described Samuel Taylor Coleridge (1772–1834):

Coleridge is the supreme tragedy of indiscipline. Never did so great a mind produce so little. He left Cambridge University to join the army; he returned to Oxford and left without a degree. He began a paper called *The Watchman* which lived for ten numbers and then died. It has been said of him: "He lost himself in visions of work to be done, that always remained to be done. Coleridge had every poetic gift but one—the gift of sustained and concentrated effort."

In his head and in his mind he had all kinds of books, as he said, himself: "[I'm] sending to the press two Octavo volumes." But the books were never composed outside Coleridge's mind, because he would not face the discipline of sitting down to write them out. No one ever reached any eminence, and no one having reached it ever maintained it, without discipline.[4]

If we want to achieve anything great in this life, anything of substance for the kingdom of God, we must develop discipline. It took Dr. Jonas Salk three long, hard years before he developed the vaccine against polio.[5] Einstein, probably the greatest scientist since Isaac Newton, once said: "I think and think for months, for years; 99 times the conclusion is false. The hundredth time I am right."[6]

About such examples Stanley Baldwin wrote: "Perseverance is basically an active trait. One is doing something and encounters difficulty in continuing it or in seeing it through to a conclusion, but he sticks with the task."[7]

Do the common work in an uncommonly good way. No plan will work unless you work.

—John D. Rockefeller, Sr.

Bloom Where You Are Planted

Sometimes people lack diligence because they aspire to be somewhere else, doing something else. They haven't learned the wisdom of the old adage, "Bloom where you are planted." Consider the case of a seminary grad who did just that.

Years ago there was a young man in seminary who wanted to serve God on the mission field. He applied to work in the country that is today Zaire (then it was the Belgian Congo). And he looked forward to service there on the continent of Africa, if that was God's will. Meanwhile, the dean at the seminary advised him to start looking for a pastorate somewhere until the mission board responded. So the young man did just that and ended up as a pastor to a very small congregation, which at the time was just meeting in a room in a local school in the South. The school was not air-conditioned, and it was "blazing hot." The young man had an inauspicious start, as church attendance started to dwindle under his ministry, at least at first. Meanwhile, the mission board wrote to him and turned him down for service because of his asthma, but this young man persisted in the ministry he had at hand. By learning the basics of one-on-one witnessing (church visitation), he was able to stop his small church from bleeding to death. In fact, through lay visitation, it became one of the fastest growing

> *"I never pray for a good garden unless*
> *I have a hoe in my hand. I say, 'Lord, you*
> *send the sunshine and the showers, and*
> *I'll keep the weeds down!'"*
>
> —An effective gardener

churches in America. He then systematized the method of lay evangelization that helped turn his church around, so that other congregations could adopt the same program, which in turn helped their growth significantly. Eventually, that ministry went worldwide and has now been employed all over the globe. The man was Dr. D. James Kennedy; the church was Coral Ridge Presbyterian Church of Ft. Lauderdale; and the worldwide ministry is Evangelism Explosion, International. Interestingly, Evangelism Explosion reached into Zaire and is being utilized there. So Dr. Kennedy eventually *did* become a missionary to the former Belgian Congo in an indirect way. The purpose of this story is to encourage you to move forward. To bloom where you are planted. To persist. To persevere. "Whatever your hand finds to do, do it with all your might." Be faithful *now* with the task you have before you.

When we are young, life seems so long; but as we grow older, all of a sudden we realize that we are not going to be here forever and that time is precious. I (Kirsti) thought it was awful to be thirty-five and without any significant accomplishments. I couldn't get out of my mind something I heard on a Tom Lehrer comedy record: "It's a sobering thought that when Mozart was my age, he had been dead for at least five years!" Mozart was only thirty-four when he died—practically my age. Think of all that he did, and what have I done? One Bible verse that really helped me during that time was Psalm 138:8: "The LORD will fulfill his purpose for me." If we are willing to work and do our best in whatever He has called us to, the Lord Himself will see to it that our lives are not wasted. Because when we do what He created us to do, we are part of God's plan and coworkers in His kingdom.

> *All men were created to busy themselves with labor . . . for the common good.*
>
> —John Calvin

Jesus worked hard, and He told His disciples that work is for an appointed time, and there will come a time when the opportunity is over: "As long as it is day, we must do the work of him who sent me. Night is coming, when no one can work" (John 9:4). What is the work that God sent Jesus to do, and that He is sending us to do also? It is the work in his vineyard. It is the work of the kingdom—the spreading of the gospel and the making of disciples, the gathering in and the teaching and the serving of his people.

Paul said, "Whatever you do, work at it with all your heart, as working for the Lord, not for men" (Col. 3:23). It is teaching like this that gave rise to the Christian work ethic.

Because we know that God sees us and will reward our labor, we do not necessarily need to be rewarded here and now, nor do we need praise from men. If we know that God knows, that can be enough.

Jesus said that "whoever wants to become great among you must be your servant, and whoever wants to be first must be slave of all" (Mark 10:43). This passage has been the inspiration for much of Christian service. The whole idea of putting others first and

> *Work for the Lord, pay is small, retirement benefits are out of this world.*
>
> —A sign outside Chuck Meyer's House of Television, Phoenix, Arizona

being their servants in order to succeed in the kingdom of God is so foreign to human nature and so revolutionary that it has changed many a heart and brought many people to Christ.

When we talk about a good Christian, he or she is often referred to as a *servant* of God, and many are those who have served Him their whole life in obscurity. God knows all His people, and no one is unknown to Him. So whether God has put us in the limelight or in a secret place, all service done unto Him for his glory is beautiful to Him. And in due time, whether in this life or the next, it will be rewarded.

I (Kirsti) grew up on the south coast of Norway in a part of the country where fishing and boating are as natural as walking. When we learned to row, we were taught the importance of using both oars. If you use only one or if there is an imbalance between the two oars, you will just row in a circle. This was used in many a sermon to illustrate the relationship between working and praying. They are both important in the kingdom of God. But if you only pray and there is no work, no fruit of your prayers, it is like rowing with one oar. It is equally true that if you only work but don't pray, you will not get anywhere either. So use both oars, work and pray. "Pray as if it were all up to God. Work as if it were all up to you."

Hard work is a good habit. Some people always work hard, and they are always diligent. Others have a hard time getting down to work. Part of this is personality, but good habits or bad habits primarily are learned. And they are learned early in life. (Not that it can't ever be learned later—in case you missed it in childhood. It's just not as easy for adults to outgrow years of bad habits.) Therefore, we do our children a big favor by teaching them to work hard. And we do them a disfavor by allowing them to be lazy.

The work we do, whether it is secular or sacred, when we do it unto the Lord, we do it out of love for him. Then it does not matter who our employer is, or whether we are self-employed. When we work out of love for God, the work takes on a new meaning and it becomes easier. When we love the Lord, *His yoke is easy* and His burden is light (Matt. 11:30). In Handel's *Messiah,* the piece called "His Yoke Is Easy" is one of the hardest to sing in the whole oratorio! Could it be that Handel was trying to communicate that even though the yoke of Christ is easy and His burden is light, it is not without struggles, nor is it something we can breeze through? It takes concentration and training; it can't be done without focusing on the conductor. It is our love for the Lord that makes his burden light and not the amount of work.

Oh, do not pray for easy lives. Pray to be strong men and women. Do not pray for tasks equal to your powers. Pray for powers equal to your tasks. Then the doing of your work will be no miracle; but you shall be a miracle. Every day you shall wonder at yourself, at the richness of life which has come to you by the grace of God.

—Phillips Brooks

When we talk of diligence as a Christian virtue, we must also talk of perseverance. Jesus said in Revelation, "Be faithful, even to the point of death, and I will give you the crown of life" (Rev. 2:10b). Jesus is urging us to not give up, but to hold on a little longer. "I am coming soon. Hold on to what you have, so that no one will take your crown" (Rev. 3:11).

> *I am long on ideas, but short on time.*
> *I expect to live to be only about a hundred.*
>
> —Thomas Alva Edison

Consider the hard work required to accomplish some great things:

- It took Edward Gibbon twenty-six years to write *The Decline and Fall of the Roman Empire.*
- John Milton would wake up at 4:00 every morning in order to write *Paradise Lost,* which some critics call "the greatest epic in the English language."[8]
- Noah Webster revolutionized (and standardized) the spelling of the English language for Americans in the early nineteenth century through his dictionary. It took him thirty-six years to complete it![9]

And on and on it goes. Anything worth accomplishing takes time and hard work. Thomas Edison's point is so well-taken: "Genius is 1 percent inspiration and 99 percent perspiration."

Conclusion

When it's all said and done, there is a great need to persevere despite the opposition of others or the natural bent toward laziness we find in our hearts. We close with the words of Teddy Roosevelt and his inspirational poem, "In the Arena":

> *Time must be the servant of eternity.*
>
> —Erwin Lutzer

> It is not the critic who counts;
> Not the man who points out
> How the strong man stumbled,
> Or where the doer of deeds
> Could have done better.

The credit belongs to the man
Who is actually in the arena;
Whose face is marred
By dust and sweat and blood;
Who strives valiantly;
Who errs and comes short
Again and again;
Who knows the great enthusiasms,
The great devotions,
And spends himself in a worthy cause;
Who at best knows in the end
The triumph of high achievement;
And who at the worst
If he fails,
At least fails while daring greatly;
So that his place shall never be
With those cold and timid souls
Who know neither victory nor defeat.[10]

In short, persevere. Hang in there. There is great merit in pursuing a worthy objective with worthy motives, even if it means we have to remain "bored a little longer." And whatever your hand finds to do, do it with all your might.

Choose that employment or calling in which you may be most serviceable to God.

—Puritan writer Richard Baxter

chapter 17

A Way of Escape

Opportunity knocks only once; temptation leans on the doorbell.

—Anonymous

One day four "men of the cloth" were enjoying a frank discussion with one another about their vices. The rabbi confessed, "I like pork." The Protestant minister said, "I drink a bottle of bourbon a day." "I have a girlfriend on the side," admitted the priest. They all turned to the Baptist minister. He shrugged his shoulders and said, "Me? I like to gossip."[1]

So what are we supposed to do when temptation comes knocking? After having looked at the seven deadly sins and their spiritual counterparts, in this chapter we want to explore some key principles for victory over sin.

The Temptation of Cain

We can learn about temptation through the story of Cain and Abel, especially in the dialogue between God and Cain: "Then the

LORD said to Cain, 'Why are you angry? Why is your face downcast? If you do what is right, will you not be accepted? But if you do not do what is right, sin is crouching at your door; it desires to have you, but you must master it" (Gen. 4:6–7).

In John Steinbeck's book *East of Eden,* there are four elderly Chinese men who study the first sixteen verses of Genesis 4 for over a period of two years. Initially, they thought that God's command to Cain was that he *shalt* or that he *must* master sin. Instead they learned from the original Hebrew that it could be better translated as "thou mayest" (implying choice). Here's a passage from that novel that sums up what they learned after all their study and reflection:

> The Hebrew word *timshel*—"Thou mayest"—that gives a choice. It might be the most important word in the world. That says the way is open. That throws it right back on a man. For if it is true that "Thou mayest," it is also true that "Thou mayest not" . . . "Thou mayest." Why, that makes a man great; that gives him stature with the gods, for in his weakness and his filth and his murder of his brother, he has still the great choice.[2]

Steinbeck goes on to say that it is this choice that makes a man a man (as opposed to a beast). He is pointing out that God has given man the possibility of triumphing over sin. This possibility to triumph, this choice, is the crown of glory and honor that God has given man.

Isn't it interesting to note that when 1 John says that *if* we sin we have an advocate with the Father (1 John 2:1). It doesn't say *when* we sin, but *if.* Imagine the flight attendant of an airplane saying, "And *when* we have to make an emergency landing. . . ." Instead, they say, "And *if* we have to make an emergency landing. . . ." Yet the same book of the Bible tells us that if we claim to have no sin, we lie. So, though we sin, even as Christians, we should not come to expect it. And in Christ, we have many resources to combat sin—resources that Cain did not necessarily have. Most of all, God has given us the Holy Spirit to help us fight sin and master temptation. By His power we can be more than conquerors.

The Temptation of Joseph

The two greatest examples in Scripture of temptation that was resisted are Jesus' temptation in the desert and Joseph with Potiphar's wife. If we would but heed him, Joseph could give us "running lessons." They are among the most valuable lessons a man could ever learn!

You will recall that Joseph was sold into slavery in Egypt by his jealous brothers. Potiphar, the captain of the guard for Pharaoh, bought him and put him to work in his household. Everything Joseph touched prospered, so Potiphar put him in charge of his household. But when her husband was away, Potiphar's wife began to make advances on Joseph; he consistently resisted her. But one day she dismissed the other servants to be alone with Joseph. Now she tried to seduce him in earnest. She must have grabbed his cloak because he resisted her once again, only this time he had to flee without his cloak. She hung on to it and then pretended that he had tried to rape her. So she framed him, and Joseph was thrown into jail for this alleged crime. But he had been faithful the whole time. Even though temporarily the circumstances worked against him, in the big picture God used it for good. Within a few years, the Lord even raised Joseph up to be in charge of Egypt, second only to Pharaoh himself. I know I am speculating when I say this, but I do not think he would have been so exalted by God had he given in.

What Joseph did to resist temptation is so simple yet so profound. He fled it. If you get

> *Sin is not hurtful because it is forbidden, but it is forbidden because it's hurtful.*
>
> —Ben Franklin,
> *Poor Richard's Almanack*

tempted to drink, stay away from bars. If you get tempted to overeat, stay away from the refrigerator, as much as you can. If you get tempted to lust, stay away from the newsstand or the beach or cable TV. It's not always possible to avoid these things—how can one always avoid the refrigerator?—but as much as is appropriate, it makes sense to try to order our lives in ways in which we are unlikely to even be tempted. I call this "environmental engineering." Here is an example from my (Jerry's) life in the realm of lust: I try to keep my house completely free from any lustful stimuli. For example, an unsolicited catalogue of women's lingerie came in the mail recently. I threw it away immediately, lest it be a snare to me. Being in the garbage can, it got old food dumped on it within minutes, thus making it irretrievable.

Part of what makes resisting temptation so hard is that we want to dabble with it. But that's sort of like gently flirting with another man's wife. Franklin P. Jones said, "What makes resisting temptation difficult, for many people, is that they don't want to discourage it completely."[3] That is so true. But if you play with fire, you can expect to get burned. Josh Billings pointed out, "One-half of the trouble of this life can be traced to saying yes too quick, and not saying no soon enough."[4] If we could become more like Joseph in that we don't even entertain the possibility and we diligently flee the scene when temptation rears its ugly head, we'd go a long way in resisting temptation when it comes knocking.

The Temptation of Christ

Joseph provided a great example on fleeing temptation, but Jesus gives us the all-time model of what to do when we are tempted—and what to do *before* we are tempted: memorize and know the Scripture. That way when the devil comes knocking with his temptations, we will be ready.

Consider the awesome fact that though He was tempted, Jesus did not give in. What if He had given in? There would be no salvation! If Jesus had given in to the temptation in the desert or in to the temptation when He was praying at Gesthemane, we would be in the proverbial state of "up the river without a paddle." We would have no hope and no basis for hope. But wonder of wonders: Jesus Christ fulfilled the plan the Father gave to Him from before time.

As we pointed out in the first chapter, to be tempted is not the same as to sin. Harold L. Bussell pointed out: "It is hard for us to think that Jesus was tempted by lust, greed, power, fornication, or murder, but He was, while remaining sinless. If that is true, then temptation itself is not sin; we can be tempted and still be guiltless."[5] John Knox added, "That the Son of God was thus tempted gives instruction to us that temptations, although they be ever so grievous and fearful, do not separate us from God's favor and mercy."[6] Sometimes I have felt guilty for being tempted to sin, even though I hadn't actually given in. But this is false guilt because being tempted to sin is not the same as giving in.

> *When fleeing temptation, don't leave a forwarding address.*
>
> —R. E. Phillips

Another thing we learn about temptation from that of Christ is that we don't really know how strong temptation is until we actually try to resist it. Only then do we realize just how powerful it really is. Listen to the brilliant argument of C. S. Lewis on this matter. (Keep in mind as you read this that when he first wrote it, it was during World War II, so his reference to the German army is to the Nazis.) He wrote:

A silly idea is current that good people do not know what temptation means. This is an obvious lie. Only those who try to resist temptation know how strong it is. After all, you find out the strength of the German army by fighting against it, not by giving in. You find out the strength of a wind by trying to walk against it, not by lying down. A man who gives in to temptation after five minutes simply does not know what it would have been like an hour later. That is why bad people, in one sense, know very little about badness. They have lived a sheltered life by always giving in. We never find out the strength of the evil impulse inside us until we try to fight it: and Christ, because He was the only man who never yielded to temptation, is also the only man who knows to the full what temptation means—the only complete realist.[7]

John MacArthur adds an interesting insight on the temptation of Christ. He says that the sword of the Spirit talked about in Ephesians 6 (the part about the armor of God) was a small sword, or a large dagger, used in hand-to-hand combat. MacArthur said that using the sword of the Spirit in spiritual combat means using specific verses to fight with the specific temptations that come your way. How did Jesus respond to the evil one when he tempted Him? With logic? With rational arguments? By making out a pro and con sheet? He fought against the devil's temptations with the Word of God: "It is written." This means that He had taken the time to learn the Word of God, to memorize portions of it, and to meditate on it and learn its meaning. We should do likewise.

If you struggle with any one or more of the seven deadly sins—and who doesn't?—I suggest you take the time to memorize one or more of the Scriptures related to that sin. Hopefully, even within the text of this book, there are plenty to choose from. Do it now, while you are *not* in a state of temptation. Richard Exley pointed out in his book *Deliver Me* (a book about temptation): "Only a fool would try to dig a storm cellar in the middle of a tornado, yet many seem to think nothing of ignoring the reality of temptation until they are in the midst of it."[8] Why not consider the goal of memorizing a verse each Sabbath? Before you know it, you'll be battle-ready before the battle comes.

Jesus was not finished with temptation after the desert experience. The devil left Him for a while, but another opportune moment came at Cesarea Philippi—just after Peter's grand confession that Jesus is the Christ. Our Lord started to talk about His suffering and death. Peter took Him aside and said: "Never, Lord! . . . This shall never happen to you!" (Matt. 16:22). We can assume that Peter was well-meaning; he was horrified that such a thing should happen to his master. The Swedish theologian Bo Giertz explained what was happening:

> Jesus answers, "Away from me Satan." That sounds terrible [that it was said to Peter], but it was true. It was the Tempter who stepped forward again—he whom Jesus had answered: "Away from me Satan" now came back with the same kind of temptation, as the first one in the desert. . . . The tempter does not use a direct evil. It is not a question of something God has forbidden. What he is suggesting is reasonable and "loving." If Jesus is the Son of God, why should He go around in the desert hungry as a lost beggar? It could not possibly be the plan that He should "suffer much and die"—if He has a good and merciful Father in Heaven.
>
> This is one of the devil's big opportunities; to appeal to what we feel is right and reasonable with the shortsighted vision that we humans have.[9]

The "prove-it" temptation also came back later. *"If* you are the Son of God. . . ." When Christ experienced the agony of the cross, this temptation was repeated. *"If* you are the king of the Jews, save yourself" (Luke 23:37). So we see that even to the very end, the devil tried to get to Jesus, but He kept resisting and won eternal victory over the devil and all his demons. Jesus took the sting out of death and the terror from the grave and triumphed over all evil.

Some people are disappointed that they never outgrow temptation. But did our Lord? Harold L. Bussell wrote:

> I have met many people who are distressed because they have not reached a point of spiritual maturity beyond temptation. They feel that they somehow have not proved themselves truly "spiritual." They hope to soar, like Jonathan Livingston Seagull, beyond all limits of reality—beyond conflict, struggle, and pain. But

> Jesus never got beyond the possibility of temptation,
> and neither will we. We all face similar conflicts.[10]

So, whether you've been a Christian for five years, twenty-five years, fifty-five years, or ninety-five years, you *can* expect temptation to come knocking. But God will always provide a way of escape. The good thing is that the less you give in, the stronger you grow in ability to resist that same area next time. And pretty soon victory (in that area) becomes autopilot. As Ben Franklin once said, "'Tis easier to suppress the first desire, than to satisfy all that follow it."[11] But be wary, lest you become arrogant and assume that you can withstand temptation in your own power (without divine help).

One thing I'll bet that God hates is the arrogance you can find among some fruitless, professing Christians. They almost seem to presume upon the grace of God, as if "God is in the forgiving business" and they can live like they please with no reference to Him but still assume they are saved.

On the other extreme are the people who think they can lose your salvation, so they "get saved" every other week. A few years ago I heard about a man, a pastor in a holiness church, who "got saved every Saturday night." Meanwhile, he was beating his wife and family. Providentially, he came to a true saving knowledge of Christ, came to understand he was saved once and for all, and he hasn't abused his wife for years now.

Holiness vs. Worldliness

Jesus said we are to be in the world but not of it. But too often too many Christians are *of* the world. As *Our Daily Bread* once put it, "God put the church in the world; Satan tries to put the world in the church."[12] J. I. Packer pointed out in his book, *Hot Tub Religion:* "Hedonism (the pleasure-seeking syndrome) bends holiness out of shape, and hedonism today has a very tight hold on our priorities."[13]

How beautiful holiness is when it is put into practice without pretense. I (Jerry) remember that before I was converted, I saw the beauty of the godly in an ungodly society. I was a freshman in college at Tulane University in a very hedonistic and secular environment, where there were beer parties everywhere and strip joints in the heart of town, which were

> *Few speed records are broken when people run from temptation.*
>
> —E. C. McKenzie

visited often by students (including once or twice by this one). There were drugs and pornography. Then there were students who worked hard for one ambition: money. In the midst of all this, I stumbled across a group of godly students, who shone like lights in the darkness. They were part of the InterVarsity group. They knew what they believed, they knew why they believed, and they knew in *whom* they believed. Their godliness was attractive to me. C. S. Lewis once said: "How little people know who think that holiness is dull. When one meets the real thing . . . it is irresistible."[14]

Worldliness dulls our spirituality. It tarnishes our holiness. The more we give in to temptation, the less we become sensitive to the Lord. The world is at enmity with the Lord. To love the world is to hate God, so says James. You can play church all you want, but if you love the world, then how can you say you love God? You're deluding yourself. J. I. Packer called the modern-day worldliness that he finds so rampant in today's church "hot tub religion." He wrote:

> Now we can see hot tub religion for what it is— Christianity corrupted by the passion for pleasure. Hot tub religion is Christianity trying to beat materialism, Freudianism, humanism, and Hollywood at their own game, rather than challenge the errors that the rules of that game reflect. "The place for the ship is in the sea," said D. L. Moody, speaking of the church and the world. "But God help the ship if the sea gets into it." His sentiment was surely just.[15]

R. C. Sproul said this about sin: "Sin is cosmic treason. Sin is treason against a perfectly pure sovereign."[16]

Resources Available to Us to Help Us Resist Temptation

What is the secret of sanctification? It would seem to me that the answer is not a "secret" at all. As we've said repeatedly, it's the Word of God. Jesus prayed to this effect: "Sanctify them by the truth; Thy word is truth." Psalm 119 says the way a young man can keep himself pure is by hiding God's Word in his heart.

Another resource to keep us from sin is fellowship with one another, especially if accountability can be a part of that equation. Fellowship has been defined as fellow Christians who are, if you will, in the same ship. We are told not to forsake assembling together—in other words, not to miss going to church. Furthermore, get plugged into some sort of Bible study or group of Christians with realistic give-and-take about our struggles. Breaking this down even further, perhaps we could find a prayer partner to whom we can hold each other accountable—with all candor. On my radio call-in show recently, we talked about temptation, and someone called in and mentioned his struggle with computer porn. I asked him about accountability, and he said it didn't work because he lied to the gentleman. Obviously, we must be honest with each other, or accountability is worthless.

> *Nothing makes it easier to resist temptation than a proper upbringing, a sound set of values, and witnesses.*
>
> —Franklin P. Jones

As Christians our ultimate resource is the Holy Spirit. But not accessing His divine power, or short-circuiting it by our sins, is like the homeless man who died on the streets of Los Angeles a few years ago, even though he had $200,000 in the bank.[17]

The power available to us through the Holy Spirit, through Christ in us, is no minor point. Seminary professor G. Manford Gutzke wrote:

> I used to think that being a Christian was a matter of clenching one's fists, gritting one's teeth, jutting out one's jaw, and being so strong that you would not fall. But the bigger you are, the harder you fall. Just making up your mind that you are going to walk is not going to hold you up on a slippery road; and many a person, whether man or woman, has found this out, with great distress. But if "underneath are the everlasting arms," if He takes hold of you by the hand, even if your feet do slip, He will not let you go. It is not just an outward, external thing, *He is in you.* It's "Christ in you, the hope of glory." This is what is made possible by the dwelling of the Holy Spirit.[18]

One Puritan writer (Golbourn) pointed out that a bird imprisoned in a cage might beat itself silly by self-efforts to get out of the pen. "If it did so, it would ere long fall back breathless and exhausted, faint and sore, and despairing."[19] The same is true of a soul that tries by self-effort to change. Instead, we are to depend on Christ. The key to sanctification is yielding yourself to God.

> *Temptations, unlike opportunities, will always give you a second chance.*
>
> —O. A. Battista

God has given us two means of grace to help us on our way to heaven—the Word and the sacraments. By reading His Word regularly and taking communion, we keep close to our Lord.

When Temptation Comes Knocking

So, putting all these thoughts together, what do we do when temptation comes knocking?

- *Flee.* Leave the scene. Turn off the TV set. Close the book. Do whatever it takes.
- *Quote and apply relevant Scripture.* Read the Bible. Use a concordance if necessary.
- *Call a trusted friend.* Ask him or her to pray with you and to call you tomorrow to make sure you did not fall today. I say "trusted" for obvious reasons. You don't want your pet sin known all over the church.
- *Pray.* Ask for divine help. I'm reminded of the story of the little boy who was trying to save up his pennies to buy a baseball bat. One night his mother overheard him praying, "O Lord, please help me save my money for a baseball bat. And, God, don't let the ice cream man come down this street!"[20]
- *When you pray, ask Jesus for help.* He's the only person in the history of the world who has been tempted and yet who passed the test unscathed, and he stands ready to assist us as we go through temptation.

And don't forget what we can do *in advance* of temptation knocking:

- Go to church on a regular basis. Be in fellowship with committed believers.
- Find a friend or group that will hold you accountable.
- Memorize key passages of Scripture dealing with your "issues."
- Do environmental engineering in your life to cut things out that will trigger temptation. For some people that may mean getting a porn-block program on the Internet. For someone else, it may mean taking a different route home each night to avoid the temptation to stop at the tavern. For someone else it may mean ridding your house of sugar

products. For someone else it may mean giving something away, just to cultivate a more generous spirit (if greed is your issue). For someone else, it may mean throwing away a slick, glossy catalogue of worthy products (that are way beyond your budget at this time). Ask the Holy Spirit to guide you if you need to do some environmental engineering where you live.

Keep in mind in all this that temptation doesn't usually come with trumpet fanfare. In his book *Deliver Me,* Richard Exley told about an associate pastor at an evangelical church who embezzled $42,000 from the church and wound up in prison. Had the devil come to him with the temptation to steal forty-two grand, he would have resisted it instantly for what it was. But it all began in a very small way, when he borrowed a twenty-dollar bill from the offerings he had access to. Initially, he borrowed the money and paid it back. Then he did it again. Then he borrowed yet another twenty with the intention of paying it back, but he wasn't able to repay. After a while, pilfering that twenty dollars stretched into stealing $42,000![21] I (Kirsti) remember when a campus minister said that the devil's strategy for trying to get you to fall away may just as well be a fifteen-year plan as a two-day one. And it all began when it was least expected.

> *Temptation, if not resisted, soon becomes necessity. Watch out for temptation—the more you see of it, the better it looks!*
>
> —Anonymous

We should try to come up with our game plan of what to do when tempted *before* temptation strikes. Bussell had this to say:

We may be tempted when we least expect it. Adam and Eve passed that special tree every day. Yet, as James Stalker writes, "One of the chief powers of temptation is

the power of surprise. It comes when you are not looking for it; it comes from the person and the quarter you
least suspect. . . . No bell rings in the sky to give warning that the hour of destiny has come."[22]

Note also the timing of temptation: "Temptation often comes not at our
strongest, but our weakest moments. When we are at the limit of our
patience, love, etc., we are tempted to be unchristian, beware. Jesus'
temptation began *after* 40 days of fasting."[23]

Conclusion

Often we hear the expression "the real world." Sometimes
Christians are told, "Will you get with it and acknowledge 'the real
world'?"—a term synonymous with the seamy side of life. The
implication is that spiritually minded Christians aren't living in the
real world. Well, let's set the
record straight. There are two
ultimate real worlds: heaven
and hell. That's it. Every decision we make must be made in
the light of eternity: our spiritual commitments, our marital
choices, our vocations, how we
spend our money. If we are
wise, we will live according to eternity.

> *Every moment of
> resistance to
> temptation is a
> victory.*
>
> —Anonymous

I close with the insights of Swedish theologian Bo Giertz, who
points out that not only should we remember the role of the devil
in the tempting we experience but also we must pray that in no
way do we participate in tempting other people. It's a sobering
thought to ponder:

Temptations do come to us all on a small or on a
grand scale. But God is not the one who tempts us (nor
can He be tempted by evil). The Tempter's dirty finger-
prints are left in our own nature. We have an inborn
egotism and self-gratification that come quite naturally.

The Tempter can always find something in us which agrees with him; therefore, he can, without difficulty, weave himself workers among us. The words of Christ are quite serious: "Woe to the man who leads astray one of these little ones who believes in me." Our first question should be: Lord, it isn't me, is it? Could I by my words or deeds cause anybody else to sin? God forbid it! Could I on any occasion be a co-worker with the devil in turning others away from Him? May it never happen, and may God stop me if I ever cause anyone to sin.[24]

chapter 18

And Forgive Us Our Debts

*When you are forgiven, someone must pay,
and the one who forgives
is the one who suffers.*

—Edwin Orr

Have you ever noticed that in cartoons when anybody dies, they all end up on clouds, plucking harps—no matter how bad they've been? A lot of people in our culture believe that everyone goes to heaven when they die, except, of course, for the really bad guys, like Hitler and Al Capone. But is that really the case?

Now that we've considered temptation and some of the key sins to avoid and some of the key virtues to embrace, let's consider the matter of forgiveness—especially the issue of how we can be forgiven even if we've given in to temptation many times. How does it work? What can we do to be forgiven for our sins? How can our consciences ever be truly cleansed?

The Centrality of the Cross

The only place anybody can get an absolution is at the cross. Throughout the ages people have sought to free themselves of their guilt in so many ways, but only one thing works. The only one capable of taking away guilt and proclaiming the sinner clean and guiltless is Jesus Christ. He is our advocate with the Father. He is the one who has power on earth to forgive sins. Why? Because of His death on the cross. Many others have suffered terrible torture and death. But the reason the death of Jesus Christ is so powerful is that He was God and He was man at the same time. He was totally sinless. He could atone for peoples' sins because He had no sin of His own, and because He was God.

> *Come to me all you who are weary and burdened, and I will give you rest.*
>
> —Jesus Christ, Matthew 11:28

God has proclaimed from ancient times (Lev. 17) that without the shedding of blood there is no forgiveness for sins. The Old Testament's sacrifices of bulls and lambs were all just a picture of the one sacrifice to come. John the Baptist said this when he saw Jesus coming: "Behold! The Lamb of God who takes away the sin of the world" (John 1:29, NKJV). So it is the blood of Christ that removes the guilt from us; it is His death that gives us life. As the prophet Isaiah said in this well-known messianic passage:

> Surely he took up our infirmities
>   and carried our sorrows,
> yet we considered him stricken by God,
>   smitten by him, and afflicted.
> But he was pierced for our transgressions,
>   he was crushed for our iniquities;
> the punishment that brought us peace was upon him,
>   and by his wounds we are healed.
> We all, like sheep, have gone astray,

> each of us turned to his own way;
> and the LORD has laid on him
>   the iniquity of us all (Isa. 53:4–6).

The Lord is merciful and slow to anger. He forgives our sins, and He does not even remember them anymore (talk about "forgive and forget"). With God there is full and absolute forgiveness. All we have to do is come to Him and ask; we have to humble ourselves before Him. We have to acknowledge our sins and turn from them. We have to give God our lives, our hearts, and our souls—through faith in Jesus Christ. He in turn gives it all back to us to make us free and whole and perfect in His sight. What an exchange: we give Him our sin; He gives us forgiveness, the cleansing of our hearts, and eternal life!

> *Without the shedding of blood there is no forgiveness.*
>
> —Hebrews 9:22b

This wonderful transformation is called justification. It is like a court decision—God as judge is declaring us not guilty of sin—not because we haven't sinned but because the righteousness of Christ is legally imputed upon us. The whole thing is based on Christ's death. If He hadn't died, there would be no opportunity to be justified. When we are justified, God looks down at us and no longer sees our sin. Instead He sees the perfect righteousness of Christ imputed onto us.

A Bare Outline of the Good News

Consider a few basics (and I'm indebted to D. James Kennedy and his classic book, *Evangelism Explosion,* for these):

- Heaven is a free gift. It is not earned or deserved. "For by grace you have been saved through faith, and that not of yourselves; it is a gift of God, not of works, lest anyone should boast" (Eph. 2:8–9, NKJV).
- Man is a sinner and cannot save himself.

- God is loving and He is holy. He will not forgive sin, unless there's a sacrifice for it. There's only one sacrifice for sin that He accepts.
- Jesus the infinite God-man paid the one and only sacrifice for sins that God accepts.
- We need to accept Jesus as our Savior and Lord. We need to have "saving faith," in which we trust in Him for our salvation and not in ourselves.
- When we accept Him, good works follow. Good works, acts of charity, and love in His name are natural consequence to knowing Christ. But we are not saved by good works. Heaven is a free gift. It is not earned or deserved. . . . (Now we're back to point one again.)[1]

Accepting the Free Gift of Salvation

Now the key question is, have *you* ever truly accepted the free gift of salvation that Jesus offers us because He died for us in our place? Have you ever sincerely repented from your sins (turned away from them—or even asked God's help to turn away from them?). Have you sincerely asked Christ to be your Savior and Lord? Do you know Him personally in your heart? If not, you can. I suggest you take a moment and say a prayer like this:

> *When God **justified** me, He made it **just**-as-**if-I'd** never sinned!*

Lord Jesus Christ, I come to You right now. I confess that I have violated Your holy law. I have given in to temptation on way too many occasions. I am sorry. Right now, by faith, I receive the free gift of salvation that cost You Your life. Thank You for dying on the cross for me, in my place. Thank You for making salvation possible through that horrible death. I ask, dear

> Lord, that You come into my heart and change me from
> the inside out. In Your name, I pray. Amen.

If that prayer reflected the true desire of your heart, then this marks
the beginning of your new life in Christ.

Key Steps to Follow

There are certain disciplines that should be followed by all
Christians, whether they are five or 105:

- *Read the Bible every day.* Study it. Memorize key verses.
  Seek to apply it in your life.
- *Pray daily.* "Be joyful always; pray continually; give thanks
  in all circumstances, for this is God's will for you in Christ
  Jesus" (1 Thess. 5:16–18).
- *Get plugged in to a local, Bible-believing church, where
  Jesus is preached.* Seek out some good friends in that
  church so that you can help one another walk with
  Christ.
- *Seek ways to "do good" in imitation of Christ.* Christianity,
  said Paul in Galatians, is faith in Christ expressing itself
  through love (Gal. 5:6).

The first step I listed above
involves the Bible. For those
not familiar with the Scriptures,
I recommend you get an easy-
to-read version. Personally, we
enjoy the NIV (the New
International Version). It's easy
to understand and was translated with the goal of strongly

> *The Bible will keep
> us from sin—or sin
> will keep us from the
> Bible!*
>
> —Anonymous

communicating God's Word in our times. You can get this in any
Christian bookstore. Many churches and ministries have copies of
the Bible that are free for the asking.

I recommend you begin by reading the fourth book of the New

Testament, which is John (as in the gospel according to John). That is a great place to start.

If you would like a free book that helps you understand the basics of the Christian life and that includes the Gospel of John in the NIV, then write to Dr. D. James Kennedy and ask for his book, *Beginning Again.*[2]

Beyond the Beginning

A beginning is just that. A beginning. Now we must move beyond that. Justification is the start of the Christian life, but it is only the start. As Christians we walk in daily repentance and daily forgiveness. God's mercy is new every morning. He lets us start over again with a clean slate. What keeps us close to the Lord and safe from all evil? It is the daily cleansing of our souls. It is the intimate fellowship with Him, which only can take place when we have no unconfessed sin in our life. Sin separates us from Him.

What are we to do when we have sinned? In spite of all our struggles against sin, we do find ourselves again and again in need of forgiveness. Every day we have to confess our sins to God. Every night before we go to sleep we need His cleansing power in our souls. Soon after we offend them, we need to ask the people around us for forgiveness to keep our relationships strong and pure.

> *Confession is good for the soul. But it may be terrible for the reputation!*
>
> —Anonymous

The Contrast of Peter and Judas

In the matter of divine forgiveness, there's an interesting contrast between Peter and Judas. Peter denied that he knew the Lord. Not only once, but three times. Judas betrayed Jesus. Both of them had committed a grievous sin against their Lord and master. What did Peter do when he realized what he had done? He went out and wept bitterly. He was sorry for his sins. What did Judas do? He was so sorry he wanted to die. He took the money he received for his betrayal and brought it back to the temple. He confessed his sin before the priest and the Pharisees. He was so remorseful and so sorry for what he had done that he went and hung himself. You can't get more sorry than that. But what was the difference? Why was Peter forgiven and restored to fellowship with Christ and the other disciples?

The key is not the amount of grief over our sin, nor is it the acknowledgment of wrongdoing—even though both of these elements are necessary for true repentance. It is simply coming to the Lord and asking His forgiveness. We do not know what took place at that first meeting between Peter and Jesus on that first Easter, but we are witnesses to what happened by the Sea of Galilee when Jesus restored and reinstated Peter. Peter went to Jesus. He came to the Lord with his sins and his grief. That takes faith. Without faith, it is not possible to come to Him, and without coming, it is not possible to receive His forgiveness.

Don't Ever Presume on the Grace of God

I have heard "Christians" say: "It doesn't matter if I do this sin, I can just ask forgiveness afterwards." This is to trample on the blood of the Son of Man. Listen to the stern warning from the book of Hebrews:

> If we deliberately keep on sinning after we have received the truth, no sacrifice for sins is left, but only a fearful expectation of judgment and of raging fire that will consume the enemies of God. Anyone who rejected the law of Moses died without mercy on the testimony of two or three witnesses. How much more severely do you think a man deserves to be punished who has trampled the Son of God under foot, who has treated as an unholy thing the blood of the covenant that sanctified

him, and who has insulted the Spirit of grace? (Heb. 10:26–29).

We have included this whole passage so that we can understand that there is no such thing as "cheap grace." Even though our salvation is free to us, it was bought at an extremely high price, and we should never take our forgiveness for granted. We need to mention here that by "deliberate" sinning, it means premeditated and planned acts of wrongdoing, and not the spontaneous fall into sin that is so common in the Christian life. God forgives everyone who comes to Him in repentance and sorrow. But when we presume upon God's grace and deliberately sin (especially making a habit of it), we become hardened in our hearts, and we begin to justify our sin and not even think we need to ask for forgiveness. Eventually we can become unable to do so.

I think it's only fair to point out that if some sensitive reader wonders if they have committed such a presumptuous sin and if so they feel sorry for it (not the consequences of it but for having offended a holy God), their sorrow alone and their desire not to continue in such sin is an indication that they are probably not guilty of "trampling the Son of God underfoot." In other words, the writer of Hebrews is condemning the professing Christian who nonchalantly continues in their sin as if it doesn't matter because they're forgiven no matter what. They presume on the grace of God, and by doing so they reveal that they've never understood His grace in the first

> *Pride was the sin of the angels in heaven.*
>
> —Anonymous

place. Presumption gets back to the sin of pride, of which we spoke in depth earlier. I'm reminded of a funeral I heard about of a 50-year-old man who lived like the devil all his life (including the end). Yet he was being eulogized as being up in heaven because when he was eighteen he had once walked down the aisle to accept the gospel! Faith without works is dead. If the man's faith had been real, it would have manifested itself at least in some ways.

Our pastor, Dr. James Kennedy, told a story of an old theologian sitting in his study at the end of his life, confessing that he had let a sin into his life when he was much younger. Of course, he had every intention of repenting and turning from it—just not yet. Over the years the sin gained such power over him that now he neither wished to nor *could he* turn from his sin, and he knew that hell awaited him, and he was powerless to do anything about it.

The Need for Regular Confession

What are we to do when we have failed the Lord? When we feel so terrible about what we have done, then what? "But if anybody does sin, we have one who speaks to the Father in our defense—Jesus Christ, the Righteous One. He is the atoning sacrifice for our sins" (1 John 2:1–2).

When we have recognized our sin, confessed it to the Lord, and asked His forgiveness, there might be another step to take. Sometimes our sins also affect other people, and we need to make it up to them. We have to go to them and ask their forgiveness. If property was lost or damaged, we have to replace it or at least offer to replace it. If there were lies or deceit, it has to be cleared up and the truth told.

One time when I (Kirsti) was in second grade, each student in my class had gotten a new box of crayons. My blue crayon broke, and it looked bad in that new box. So I took the blue crayon from the box of one of the other girls when she was not looking. Every time I opened my crayon box and saw the whole blue crayon, I was reminded of what I had done. Soon it was all I could think about. I told my mother what I had done. My mom said that this made me a thief and that I needed to confess it to God and promise Him that I wouldn't steal anymore. We also went to the store and bought a new pack of crayons, and I had to go to the house of that girl. By myself, I had to ring the doorbell and explain what I had done, ask her forgiveness, and then give her the box of new crayons. I still remember the feeling of dread in the pit of my stomach, and when-

> *"Come now, let us reason together,"*
>   *says the LORD.*
> *"Though your sins are like scarlet,*
>   *they shall be white as snow;*
> *though they are red as crimson,*
>   *they shall be like wool."*
>
> —Isaiah 1:18

ever I have been tempted to take something that wasn't mine, remembering that feeling is enough to keep me in line.

This is a small illustration of what it means to live as a Christian. It doesn't mean that we never sin. It does mean that when we do sin, we confess it to God, ask His forgiveness, and make restitution. When the Holy Spirit reminds us of a sin we have done or of something we have failed to do, it is of utmost importance that we obey Him and deal with it right away. This is living in the light; it is the only way to stay close to God and close to the people around us.

Living for Christ is a day-by-day experience. For this reason, Christians the world over will pray this day as our Lord taught us:

And forgive us our debts,

As we forgive our debtors.

And do not lead us into temptation,

But deliver us from the evil one (Matt. 6:12–13, NKJV).

When temptation comes knocking, slam the door in Satan's face. Look for it and you will find God's way of escape.

Endnotes

Chapter 1

1. C. S. Lewis, *The Screwtape Letters* (New York: Macmillan, 1961), 56. (Bracketed comment is author's.)

2. C. S. Lewis, *Mere Christianity* (New York: Macmillian, 1960), 51.

3. Cal Thomas, quoted in D. James Kennedy, host, "Character & Destiny" special on *The Coral Ridge Hour* (Ft. Lauderdale: Coral Ridge Ministries), September 1994.

4. Marion Miller, ed., *Life and Works of Abraham Lincoln: Centenary Edition,* vol. 5, (New York: The Current Literature Publishing Co., 1907), 209, (author emphasis).

5. Dave Breese, *Satan's Ten Most Believable Lies* (Chicago: Moody Press, 1974), 15.

6. Paraphrase from Erwin Lutzer, *How to Say No to a Stubborn Habit* (Wheaton: Victor Books, 1986), 35.

7. Joe Bayly, *Eternity,* April 1985.

8. Randy C. Alcorn, *Christians in the Wake of the Sexual Revolution* (Portland, Ore.: Multnomah, 1985), 15.

9. Elisabeth Elliot, *A Slow and Certain Light* (Waco, Tx.: Word, 1973), 50.

Chapter 2

1. Henry Fairlie, *The Seven Deadly Sins Today* (Washington, D.C.: New Republic Books, 1978), 7–8.

2. Quoted in ibid, 11.

Chapter 3

1. Walter B. Knight, *Knight's Treasury of Illustrations* (Grand Rapids: Wm. B. Eerdmans, 1963), 299.

2. Lewis, *Mere Christianity,* 109, 110–111.

3. *Nelson's Illustrated Bible Dictionary* (Nashville: Thomas Nelson Publishers, 1986), 126.

4. Lewis, *Mere Christianity,* 109.

5. Douglas Bush, ed., *The Complete Poetical Works of John Milton* (Boston: Houghton Mifflin, 1965), 213–215.

6. Ibid., 218.

7. Albert Speer, *Inside the Third Reich* (New York: Macmillan, 1970), 248.

8. Quoted in Herman Rauschning's Preface to Armin L. Robinson, ed., *The Ten Commandments: Ten Short Novels of Hitler's War Against the Moral Code* (New York: Simon and Schuster, 1943), xiii.

9. This quote is sometimes attributed to the captain, but historians seem to dispute that. It seems rather to have been a common expression.

10. Doug Phillips, "Titanic Chivalry," *World,* 28 March 1998, 28.

11. Anthony Hoekema, "How We See Ourselves: We must base self-image on God's love, not on our good looks," *Christianity Today,* 8 November 1985, 38.

12. Eric Liddell, "The Muscular Christianity of Eric Liddell: The Olympic runner and missionary of discipleship," *Christianity Today,* 14 June 1985, 24.

Chapter 4

1. Knight, *Illustrations,* 312–13.

2. *Nelson's Illustrated Bible Dictionary,* 497.

3. Tony Augarde, *The Oxford Dictionary of Modern Quotations* (Oxford: Oxford Univ. Press, 1991), 219:27.

4. Tom Lehrer, "National Brotherhood Week," *That Was the Year That Was,* Reprise Records, 1965, sound recording.

5. Kirsti heard this story growing up as a child in her native Norway.

6. *Webster's New Collegiate Dictionary* (Springfield, Mass.: G. & C. Merriam Co., 1954), 402.

7. Matthew Henry, *Commentary on the Whole Bible* (Grand Rapids: Zondervan, 1961), 1222.

8. Mary K. Hesson, *Coral Ridge Presbyterian Church Communicator,* May 1998, newsletter.

9. Thomas Sowell et al, *Inside American Education: The Decline, the Deception, the Dogmas* (New York: The Free Press, 1993), 3.

10. Francois de Salignac de la Mothe Fenelon, *Christian Perfection* (New York: Harper & Row, 1947), 43.

11. "Remembering Mother Teresa: Nobel Peace Prize winner 'not worthy,'" *Chicago Tribune,* reproduced in [Ft. Lauderdale] *Sun-Sentinel,* 10 September 1997, 17A.

12. Liddell, "Muscular Christianity," *Christianity Today,* 25.

Chapter 5

1. Tan, *7,700 Illustrations,* 291.

2. R. Kent Hughes, *Disciplines of a Godly Man* (Wheaton, Ill.: Crossway Books, 1991), 119.

3. Tan, *7,700 Illustrations,* 289.

4. Michael Hodgin, *1001 Humorous Illustrations for Public Speaking* (Grand Rapids: Zondervan, 1994), 172.

5. Knight, *Illustrations,* 134.

6. Ibid.

7. I'm indebted for this list of Scriptures to Mary Hunt, *The Financially Confident Woman* (Nashville: Broadman & Holman, 1996), 105. She lists even more.

8. Henry, *Commentary,* 1339–40.

9. Hunt, *The Financially Confident Woman,* 105.

10. Ibid., 107.

11. Richard A. Swenson, *Margin: Restoring Emotional, Physical, Financial, and Time Reserves to Overloaded Lives* (Colorado Springs: NavPress, 1992), 165.

12. James Dean and Charles Morris, *Breaking Out of Plastic Prison* (Grand Rapids: Fleming H. Revell, 1997), 17.

13. Tom Lehrer, "A Christmas Carol," *An Evening (Wasted) with Tom Lehrer,* Reprise Records, 1959, sound recording.

14. Ralph Winter, "Missions Movement: War-time Lifestyle," *Christian History,* Vol. VI, No. 2, 30, (author emphasis).

15. "Lines from Our Times," *U. S. News & World Report,* 9 January 1989, 67.

16. "Happiness is . . ." [Ft. Lauderdale] *Sun-Sentinel,* 10 June 1987.

Chapter 6

1. Joey Adams, *The God Bit* (New York: Mason & Lipscomb, 1974), 183.

2. *The Cheapskate Monthly* is a newsletter published to encourage financial confidence and responsible spending. Its address: P. O. Box 2135, Paramount, CA 90723.

3. Hunt, *The Financially Confident Woman,* 10.

4. Ibid., 19.

5. Dean and Morris, *Breaking Out of Plastic Prison,* 14.

6. Ibid., 16.

7. Ibid., 17.

8. Larry Burkett, *Debt-Free Living: How to Get Out of Debt (and Stay Out)* (Chicago: Moody Press, 1989), 13–15.

9. Ron Blue, *Master Your Money* (Nashville: Thomas Nelson, 1991), 20–23, 35, 60.

10. Ibid., 61.

11. Larry Burkett, *How to Manage Your Money* (Chicago: Moody Press, 1975), 13.

12. W. T. Purkiser, "Thanksgiving: The Memory of the Heart," *Signs of the Times,* November 1986, 23.

13. Hodgin, *1001 Humorous Illustrations,* 317.

14. Swenson, *Margin,* 190.

15. Knight, *Knight's Book of Illustrations,* 371–72.

16. *Washington Times,* 17 November 1986.

17. John Powell, S. J., *He Touched Me* (Niles, Ill.: Argus Communications, 1974), 30.

Chapter 7

1. This took place at Thomas Jefferson High School, Port Arthur, Tex., early 1960s, while a friend of ours was a French teacher there.

2. Thankfully, this man became born again and after his prison term went back to make peace with the pharmacist. D. James Kennedy, host, "Character and Destiny," *The Coral Ridge Hour,* September 1994, television program.

3. I'm borrowing a phrase from George Bailey, played by Jimmy Stewart, in Frank Capra's *It's a Wonderful Life,* when George was rebuking Mr. Henry F. Potter, a miserable man consumed with greed and envy.

4. Ralph B. Hupka, "The Motive for the Arousal of Romantic Jealousy: Its Cultural Origin" in Peter Salovey, ed., *The Psychology of Jealousy and Envy* (New York: The Guildford Press, 1991), 258–59.

5. Quoted in Richard H. Smith, "Envy and the Sense of Injustice" in Salovey, *Psychology of Jealousy and Envy,* 79.

6. Ibid., 81.

7. Ibid., 81–82.

8. Ibid., 82.

9. Betsy Cohen, *The Snow White Syndrome: All about Envy* (New York: Macmillan, 1986), 17.

10. *Webster's Third New International Dictionary* (Springfield, Mass., 1961).

11. William James, *The Principles of Psychology* (Cambridge, Mass.: Harvard Univ., 1890, 1983), 271.

Chapter 8

1. Will Durant, *Caesar and Christ: A History of Roman Civilization and of Christianity from Their Beginnings to A.D. 325* (New York: Simon and Schuster, 1972), 71.

2. Robin Lane Fox, *Pagans and Christians* (San Francisco: Harper & Row, 1986), 47.

3. Quoted in ibid., 324.

4. Durant, *Caesar and Christ,* 652.

5. David B. Barrett and Todd M. Johnson, *Our Globe and How to Reach It* (Birmingham, Ala.: New Hope, 1990), 57.

Chapter 9

1. "Merrill Lynch Branch Manager Slain," *The Miami Herald,* 27 October 1987, 1, 10.

2. Harriet Goldhor Lerner, *The Dance of Anger* (New York: Harper & Row, 1985), 1.

3. *Nelson's Illustrated Bible Dictionary,* 725.

4. *Webster's New World Dictionary of the Americas: College Edition,* 56.

5. Tan, *7,700 Illustrations,* 132.

6. Ibid.

7. Ibid.

8. James C. Hefley, quoted in ibid.

9. Mike Cooper, "Expressing Anger Increases Stroke Risk—Study," Orlando, FL (Reuters), 11 November 1997, 1:54 AM EST.

10. Ibid.

11. Dale Carnegie, *How to Stop Worrying and Start Living* (New York: Simon and Schuster, 1948), 101–02.

12. Robert Stack, *Unsolved Mysteries,* CBS-TV, 29 May 1998.

13. Theodore Isaac Rubin, *The Angry Book* (New York: Collier, 1970), 170.

14. Tan, *7,700 Illustrations,* 133.

15. *Unsolved Mysteries,* CBS-TV, 29 May 1998.

16. Rubin, *The Angry Book, 170.*

17. "Multiple wounds killed Phil Hartman," Associated Press, 30 May 1998.

18. "Lady-Killer," *Serial Killers* (New York: Time-Life Books, 1992), 11.

Chapter 10

1. John Nieder and Thomas Thompson, *Forgive and Love Again* (Eugene, Ore.: Harvest House, 1991), 48.

2. Walter A. Elwell, *Baker Encyclopedia of the Bible,* vol. 1 (Grand Rapids, Mich.: Baker Book House, 1988), 810.

3. Nieder and Thompson, *Forgive and Love Again,* 40–41.

4. Margaret Jensen, *First We Have Coffee* (San Bernadino, Calif.: Here's Life Publishers, 1982).

5. Vera Sinton, *How Can I Forgive?* (Oxford: Lyon Press, 1990), 7.

6. Knight, *Treasury of Illustrations,* 133.

7. Sinton, *How Can I Forgive?,* 7.

8. Joseph Exell, gen. ed., *The Biblical Illustrator* (Grand Rapids, Mich.: Baker Book House, 1973), 79.

Chapter 11

1. Laurie Hall, *An Affair of the Mind* (Colorado Springs, Colo.: Focus on the Family, 1996), 99.

2. Ibid., 100.

3. Ibid., 98–99.

4. Lewis, *Mere Christianity,* 89.

5. Most of what I'm saying here is geared toward heterosexuals. For those struggling with homosexuality, a number of excellent books are available, such as Joe Dallas, *Conflicts in Desire* (Eugene, Ore.: Harvest House, 1996). Those wishing to be free from homosexuality would do well to contact Exodus International at 206-784-7799.

6. Hall, *Affair,* 11.

7. Ibid.

8. Transcript from a CRM-TV interview of Ted Baehr, conducted by Jerry Newcombe, on location in Atlanta, 5 February 1992.

9. George Barna, *The Barna Report, 1992–1993, An Annual Survey of Life-Styles, Values and Religious Views: America Renews Its Search for God* (Ventura, Calif.: Regal Books, 1992), 125.

10. There is a redemptive ray of hope in the story because Bathsheba was the mother of Solomon and Nathan and thus included in the bloodline of Christ Himself (1 Chron. 3:8 and Luke 3:31). This shows God's forgiveness and His redemptive power.

11. Robert T. Michael, John H. Gagnon, Edward O. Laumann, and Gina Kolata, *Sex in America: A Definitive Survey* (Boston: Little, Brown, 1994), 124.

12. Ibid., 112, 119, 124, 125.

13. Ibid., 89.

14. Randy Alcorn, *Sexual Revolution,* 212.

15. Quoted in Tom Minnery, ed., *Pornography: A Human Tragedy* (Wheaton, Ill.: Tyndale House, 1987), 165.

Chapter 12

1. Now some theologians believe that Romans 7 describes Paul prior to conversion. Then, when he received the Holy Spirit (which he described in Romans 8), he was able to withstand sin. Even if that interpretation is essentially the case, I still think the description of the tormented sinner who can't control himself could apply to some sincere, well-meaning Christians who have not yet managed to achieve victory over sin.

2. J. Allan Peterson, *The Myth of the Greener Grass* (Wheaton, Ill.: Tyndale House, 1983), 16–17.

3. Hughes, *Disciplines,* 23–24.

4. Dr. Donald E. Wildmon, "It Is Time to End the Religious Bigotry," *AFA Journal,* July 1995, 21.

5. Hughes, *Disciplines,* 23–24.

6. Dr. Joseph Stowell made this point on his series on temptation on *Proclaim!* on the Moody Bible Radio Network, April–May 1998.

7. Comments by Russ Johnston, How to Live by Faith Seminar, Coral Ridge Presbyterian Church, Ft. Lauderdale, Fla., 1981.

8. Michael, Gagnon, Laumann, and Kolata, *Sex in America,* 111.

9. Ibid., 127.

10. *Our Daily Bread* (Grand Rapids, Mich.: Radio Bible Class), 16 August 1982.

Chapter 13

1. Hodgin, *1001 Humorous Illustrations,* 117.

2. Study from *Science* magazine, quoted by Paul Recer, "Number of Fat Americans Increases," Associated Press, 29 May 1998.

3. Victor Buono quoted in Mary Louise Bringle, "Confessions of a Glutton," *The Christian Century,* 25 October 1989, 955.

4. Henry, *Commentary,* 192.

5. Howard Clark Kee, "Jesus: A Glutton and a Drunkard," *New Testament Studies,* 1996, 2:391.

6. "April 14," *Food for Thought,* 1980, Hazelden Educational Services, Box 176, Center City, Minn. 55012.

7. *1990 Guinness Book of World Records* (New York: Sterling), 10.

8. Bringle, "Confessions of a Glutton," 956.

9. *Encyclopedia Americana,* s.v.

10. *Webster's Third International Dictionary,* 762.

11. Bringle, "Confessions of a Glutton," 955.

12. *British Medical Journal* (Intl.), 21 December 1996, 1595–96.

13. "Mealtime on the Mason-Dixon," *Newsweek,* 6 October 1997, 8.

14. Ibid.

15. Mary K. Hesson, "Thoughts on Gluttony," unpublished, 23 May 1998.

Chapter 14

1. George Bernard Shaw quoted in Augarde, *Modern Quotations,* 193.

2. Hodgin, *1001 Humorous Illustrations,* 166.

3. "The Fat Price of Dieting," *Kiplinger's Finance Magazine,* January 1993.

4. S. I. McMillen, M.D., and David Stern, *None of These Diseases* (Old Tappan, N.J.: Fleming H. Revell, 1963, 1984), 146.

5. Ibid., 145.

6. "Hollywood Takes It Off," *People,* 13 January 1992.

7. Delta Burke, excerpt from *Delta Style: Eve Wasn't a Size 6 (and Neither Am I)* (New York: St. Martin's Press), excerpted in *People,* 3 March 1998.

8. "By Design," *People,* 3 March 1998.

9. *Evangelical Dictionary of Theology* (Grand Rapids, Mich.: Baker Book House, 1984), 400.

10. "Russian Fasting Tradition," *Russian Life,* March 1997.

11. Quoted in "Christian Diets Point to Getting 'Slim for Him,'" *National Catholic Reporter,* 12 December 1997.

12. Neva Coyle and Marie Chapin, *Free to be Thin* (Minneapolis: Bethany House, 1998).

13. Ibid., 201.

14. Carole Lewis with Terry Whalin, *First Place* (Nashville: Broadman & Holman, 1998).

15. Ibid., 18.

16. Gwen Shamblin, *The Weigh Down Diet* (New York: Doubleday, 1997).

17. In 1998 Hallelujah Acres relocated to North Carolina. You can call this number to order their books: 704–481–1700.

18. Robert S. McGee and Wm. Drew Mountcastle, *Conquering Eating Disorders* (Nashville: NewLife Press, 1993).

19. *Diagnostic and Statistical Manual of Mental Disorders,* 4th ed. (Washington, D.C.: American Psychiatry Association, 1994), 539–50.

20. Mary K. Hesson, "Self-Control for Foods Addicts Is Possible," based on an interview with Mary Kay Tortoriello, 8 June 1998. Mary Kay Tortoriello can be reached at Footprints of Hope, phone: 954-565-4643; fax: 954-565-4622.

21. Mary Kay Tortoriello, "Conquering Eating Disorders," *Footprints of Hope Newsletter,* vol. 1, no. 1.

Chapter 15

1. Walter B. Knight, *More of Knight's Timely Illustrations* (Murfreesboro, Tenn.: Sword of the Lord Publishers, 1984), 325.

2. Larry Burkett, *Whatever Happened to the American Dream?* (Chicago: Moody Press, 1993), 237.

3. D. James Kennedy and Jerry Newcombe, *What If Jesus Had Never Been Born?* (Nashville: Thomas Nelson, 1994), 110.

4. Dan Quayle and Diane Medved, *The American Family: Discovering the Values That Make Us Strong* (New York: Zondervan, 1996), 273.

5. D. James Kennedy and Jerry Newcombe, *The Gates of Hell Shall Not Prevail* (Nashville: Thomas Nelson, 1996), 187.

6. Robert MacNeil, "The Trouble with Television," *Reader's Digest,* March 1985.

7. Stanley and Patricia Gundry, *The Wit and Wisdom of D. L. Moody* (Chicago: Moody Press, 1974), 62.

8. Ibid., 64.

9. Tan, *7,700 Illustrations,* 1484.

10. Statement by Bill Bennett made on "Character and Destiny," D. James Kennedy, *The Coral Ridge Hour* (Ft. Lauderdale, September 1994), television program.

11. *Fort Lauderdale News,* October 1985.

12. [Fort Lauderdale] *News Sun-Sentinel,* 21 December 1986.

13. [Fort Lauderdale] *News Sun-Sentinel,* 3 December 1985.

14. Chuck Colson and Jack Eckerd, *Why America Doesn't Work* (Dallas: Word Books, 1991), 4.

15. Ibid., 24.

16. Quoted in Jerry Bridges, *The Pursuit of Holiness* (Colorado Springs: NavPress, 1978), 98–99.

17. David Watson, *Called and Committed: World-Changing Discipleship* (Wheaton, Ill.: Harold Shaw Publishers, 1982), 2.

18. Tan, *7,700 Illustrations,* 1630.

19. David Livingstone, quoted in Stephen Neill, *A History of Christian Missions* (New York: Penguin Books, 1977), 315.

Chapter 16

1. Paul Harvey, *Destiny* (New York: Bantam Books, 1983), 126.

2. Quoted in ibid.

3. *Washington Times,* 3 October 1992.

4. Gordon MacDonald, *Ordering Your Private World* (Nashville, Tenn.: Thomas Nelson, 1984), 70.

5. Stanley Baldwin, *How to Build Your Christian Character* (Wheaton, Ill.: Victor Books, 1983), 69.

6. Ibid.

7. Ibid., 70.

8. Kerry M. Wood, Helen McDonnell, John Pfordresher, Mary Alice Fite, and Paul Lankford, *Classics in World Literature* (Glenview, Ill.: Scott, Forseman and Company, 1989), 500.

9. Tan, *7,700 Illustrations,* 438.

10. Theodore Roosevelt, "In the Arena," quoted in Roger Ailes with Jon Kraushar, *You Are the Message* (New York: Doubleday, 1995), 39.

Chapter 17

1. Adams, *The God Bit,* 185.

2. John Steinbeck, *East of Eden* (New York: Viking Press, 1952), chapter 24, section 2. From the five-novel collection of Steinbeck books (New York: William Heinemann, Inc., 1979), 687.

3. Reagan and Phillips, *All-American Quote Book,* 299.

4. Tan, *7,700 Illustrations,* 1447.

5. Harold L. Bussell, *Lord, I Can Resist Anything but Temptation* (Grand Rapids: Zondervan, 1985), 34.

6. Ibid.

7. Lewis, *Mere Christianity*, 124–25.

8. Richard Exley, *Deliver Me* (Nashville: Thomas Nelson, 1998), inside cover flap.

9. Bo Giertz, *Å Tro På Kristus* (To Believe in Christ), passage translated by Kirsti Sæbø Newcombe (Askim, Norway: Luther Forlag, 1973, 1976), 149.

10. Bussell, *Anything but Temptation*, 37.

11. Franklin, *Poor Richard's Almanack*, 55.

12. *Our Daily Bread* (Grand Rapids: Radio Bible Class), 9 May 1980.

13. J. I. Packer, *Hot Tub Religion* (Wheaton, Ill.: Tyndale House, 1987), 68.

14. C. S. Lewis, quoted in Clyde Kilby, ed., *A Mind Awake: An Anthology of C.S. Lewis* (New York: Harcourt Brace Jovanovich, 1968), 136.

15. Packer. *Hot Tub Religion*, 85.

16. R. C. Sproul, quoted in ibid., 151.

17. [Ft. Lauderdale] *News Sun-Sentinel*, 24 December 1989.

18. George Manford Gutzke, *Plain Talk about Real Christians*.

19. *A Homiletic Encyclopedia*, 483.

20. Tan, *7,700 Illustrations*, 1445.

21. Exley, *Deliver Me*, 28–29.

22. Bussell, *Anything but Temptation*, 14.

23. Tan, *7,700 Illustrations*, 1443.

24. Giertz, *Å Tro På Kristus*, 153–54.

Chapter 18

1. D. James Kennedy, *Evangelism Explosion* (Wheaton, Ill.: Tyndale House, 1970, 1977, 1983), 16–44.

2. Write to James Kennedy, Box 40, Ft. Lauderdale, FL 33302, and ask for *Beginning Again* or call 954-772-0404.

Index